EVERYTHING ELSE

EVERYTHING ELSE

Copyright © 2014 by Brett Laxton
All rights reserved. This book or any portion thereof
may not be reproduced or used in any manner whatsoever
without the express written permission of the publisher
except for the use of brief quotations in a book review.
Printed in the United States of America

First Printing, 2014

ISBN 978-1-312-55363-7

brettlaxton@gmail.com

EVERYTHING ELSE

Thank you!

To my wife, Amy. You are the one who encouraged me to begin writing. Its your fault. Love you G.

To my kids, Tyler and Graham, because this book would be pretty short without their adventures. You two amaze me every day!

To my parents because they are about to read what really happened as I grew up. Sorry, Mom and Dad, but thanks for the great home.

To my brother for not beating me up and for always revealing the truth to me, even when the truth was too much for an eight-year-old to handle.

To Jami Hunt-Williams, a friend in college I "hired" to help me write a report. She was a professional. I got a "D" on the report. Now 16 years later, she is my creative editor. Go figure. Thanks for answering my random questions at all times of the night.

To Quigg Co. (Kenzi) Once again you have created what could not be imagined.

To Jessica Hartman, Gretchen Shaw, Wendi Stickle & Jennifer Harrison- Thanks for all of your help, beginning, middle and end! I know it was a mess.

To Jesus, because He saved me. Not only did He save me, but He also gave me purpose. He has taken this mess and made something beautiful out of it.

EVERYTHING ELSE

Table of Contents

Introduction	7
In The Beginning	11
Big Brother	15
Baseball, Slurpees & Death	17
Manliness, a Ford & a Bully	21
Bath Time, Army Men & the Family Bible	27
Vampires, Snapping Turtles & a BB Gum	33
Santa Claus, Christmas Ninjas & Grandma	37
Bathroom Breaks, Screaming & Slapping Dad	41
Mrs. Newton, Street Smarts & Mini-Mart	45
A Box, Secrets & Moonings	53
High School BFF's	61
Cornfields, a Station Wagon & Fireworks	65
A Jeep, a Lost Boy & Neighbors	71
Zippers, Dances & Graduation	77

EVERYTHING ELSE

Homecoming, a Jerk & a Girl	85
Hearing Aids, Aliens & Tumors	93
College Years	101
Amy	105
A Drunk, Bible Majors & Beauty	109
Robbers, Friends & Newlyweds	113
Bees, Lies & Nanny-Nanny Poo-Poo	121
Marriage & Family	127
Cardinals, Mud Day & a Fun Sucker	131
Momma Graham	137
The Family Dog, a Fire & Church	143
Waffles, Burps & Whoa	147
A Challenge	153

EVERYTHING ELSE

Introduction

Why in the world would anyone care what I have to say? This was the thought I had when my friend Nate told me I had to keep going. I started writing for therapy as a suggestion from my wife who is currently working on her master's in counseling. I was not surprised by her daily confirmations that I was a bit jacked up. I knew I had issues, one of them being anxiety. She treated me by prescribing one of two things: exercise or writing. I chose the latter.

I worried most about why anyone would care to read what I wrote. I am still pondering the answer to that question. So, if you are reading this, it either means you know me, you were the participant in a white elephant gift exchange or you are looking for a story.

I have always loved stories. I can remember nearly every story in my life, from the ones they make you read in school to the funny ones that just happen. Kind of like the time a man in a van almost hit my family on the streets of Savannah. Wow, I just realized that doesn't sound all that humorous, but let me explain.

We had just finished eating at The Lady and Sons, Paula Deen's restaurant. We were crossing the street, and this van whipped by, not even slowing as we were crossing the street. I grabbed my

EVERYTHING ELSE

family, and in their defense, I did what any alpha male would do to protect his tribe.

"Hey!" I yelled out as the van skidded away.

The driver stuck his head out of the van while driving and hollered back at me: "Hey, hey!" (In case this is moving too fast, that was two. Count them. TWO heys my way). No way was this guy going to get away with almost hitting my family and then two-hey-ing me.

It was the Serengeti, and it was time to climb pride rock and let this guy know who was the keeper of the kingdom. I was in touch with my inner lion. Katy Perry had nothing on me, and everyone was gonna hear me roar.

"Hey... hey... hey!" I yelled.

Right as it left my lips, I realized that as much as I wanted to be Mufasa, I was yelling out something from Fat Albert. Like other things in my life, I hadn't really thought my statement all the way through. Now I was the Alpha...Albert.

As we finished crossing the street, I heard my daughter laughingly say to my wife, "Dad just said, 'Hey, hey, hey.'" Then Graham chimed in, "Hey, hey, hey." The rest of the evening almost every response I got from my family was followed with, "Hey, hey, hey." "You want ice cream?" They would respond, "Yes, hey, hey, hey."

My life has been a culmination of stories, chapters, if you will. When you think about it, stories can stand alone, but when put together, make an even greater story. One story is really just a bunch of smaller stories tied together. You never have the privilege of understanding how important the smaller stories are until you watch them develop into something bigger, like a memoir or a biography.

What you are reading is not a biography. Biographies should be reserved for people who have invented something or broken a

EVERYTHING ELSE

record, Politicians or great humanitarians. I am none of those. I am a husband, a dad, a friend and a follower of Christ. The following pages are filled with stories. Some of them changed me, some of them shamed me, but all of them shaped me in some way.

If you are someone who loves stories, you will probably enjoy this book. If you are a person who partakes in deep, intellectual conversations and has a collection of higher-level learning degrees, you will probably understand why my wife has diagnosed me with so many disorders. As I once heard someone say, "The cookies are on the bottom shelf on this one. Anyone can understand this."

If you are a person struggling with anxiety, I suggest you follow the great advice of my wife and write or exercise. I have started both, but I enjoy writing much more than I enjoy dragging myself around a track.

So why share with you, a total stranger, the stories that are, in essence, nothing more than my personal therapy sessions? Because every story has merit, and every human being has room for a bit more merit in their lives. So as you read, consider these merits: 1. You're not so bad after all. It's true what they say about the possibility of it always being worse. 2. It is others' failures and successes that teach us to be a bit more patient with ourselves. This book contains several of my own. 3. You may or may not have played in cornfields, grown up in the 80's or had movie-worthy childhood friends, but I think you will relate.

Stories are important. Men like to pretend a movie with a great story is a bit girly, but secretly men love them. It is true of men that our stories get a little longer and a bit more epic as we tell them, and perhaps we take the center stage of our stories a little too often as well. It's hard to distance yourself from your own stories, but I swear I have at least tried to temper my stories with what is most definitely a

EVERYTHING ELSE

self-deprecating truth. I tried to remember the real heroes and the lessons I learned from them.

What about you? You have a story made of smaller stories, and people want to hear it. Actually, people need to hear it. Anybody who wants to have a relationship with us, a deep relationship, has to know our stories. Our stories reveal our character, our passions, our flaws and our sense of humor. They take you from the dad of that kid who plays on my son's baseball team to a person with a name and a place in that person's memory. A story takes us from someone we see at the mailbox to someone we know and someone we would like to get to know more.

As you read this, practice telling your stories. See what comes out in your next conversation with the guy across the street. It may be that you have more in common than a zip code. Could you have been placed on that very street with those neighbors on purpose? Could you be there to build something? Perhaps a community?

Religious or not, most of Jesus' teachings from the Bible took place through storytelling. A good story, one that is relatable, allows you to take your defenses down and see commonalities. Next thing you know, you will have more than just neighbors. You will have a community.

Don't just share stories, though. Share in the lessons we learn through storytelling. We can look out the window, keep the door shut and see our neighbors are home, know what kind of car they drive and notice they are doing some remodeling or they have out-of-town guests. But what about everything else? I challenge you as you read to look at your stories and find the everything else.

EVERYTHING ELSE

In the Beginning…

I am not sure that my first memory is the healthiest of memories. I had incredible parents: my dad worked hard in industrial work and my mom stayed home with us and took care of the house. My first memories are in the basement of that house out at Rural Route 2 D94, nestled in the cornfields of Illinois… who even uses the word nestled? My dad and uncles built that house and that makes me feel old, like I grew up on Little House on the Prairie. I mean, who builds their own house anymore?

My dad did, he drew up the blueprints, bought the supplies and spent hours after work and on weekends building a house for his family. During the early evenings or weekends my brother and I would play in the basement while my mom, dad and two uncles would work until sundown. Now here is my first memory. The concrete floors were smooth and dusty in the basement. This floor was perfect for some big wheel action. If you know what a Big Wheel is then congrats! You're old! If you don't know what a Big Wheel is,

EVERYTHING ELSE

Google it. My brother, Mark, four years older my senior, is a calculated person, one who considers the cost before making any decision and he normally makes great decisions. My brother never picked on me, I don't have any of the epic "my brother put me in a pillowcase and tied it to the family dog" anecdotes or anything like that. He was a great big brother and I was the annoying little brother. You need to remember the "great big brother" thing because my first memory is going to sound like he was being mean, but I promise you he was not. It was hours of fun.

The game was this: I would sit on the Big Wheel and Mark would stand behind me waiting as I would adjust my position and ready myself. Then he would ask "Are you ready?" He always asked the question and I always replied the same: "Yes I am!" When I would give the okay, he would run as fast as he could and push me like we were on a bobsledding team. My feet, high up in the air so they would not touch the whirling pedals spinning at lightning speed, we would fly, the plastic wheels sliding so willingly along the smooth concrete floor, the basement wall quickly approaching. As we neared the wall approaching speeds of at least 60 mph or probably six miles per hour because when you are four years old on a Big Wheel in the basement (the calculation is lost on more important things) my brother would give me one last lunge and he would let go. It was a separation much like the old NASA footage of rockets as they slowly leave land behind and break the sky… it was launch.

It was almost like I could tell when he released and pulled away from me and I was on my own… just me, the Big Wheel and speed bearing down on the concrete wall ahead. I would brace for impact because that's what I was going to get. It was the 1970's; we didn't know what helmets were, we didn't have knee pads or elbow pads, we didn't even know what the funny straps in the car were for. And the only type of protection gear I knew of was The Duke, another

EVERYTHING ELSE

1970's throwback probably responsible for protecting the ability to procreate for an entire generation of young male athletes.

It was the 70's; the era of disco and brain damage did not scare us. Our seatbelts were the powerful arms of our mothers; the real seatbelts were to keep the grocery bags from flopping onto their sides. Floor boards were made for sitting, back windows were the extra bed on long trips and if you were blessed enough to own the Holy Grail of vehicles, the station wagon, the cargo area might as well have been an extra room in your house. But back to my Big Wheel and impending doom headed for me in the form of our basement wall. I was hurling across the floor, bracing for impact and then BOOM! I would hit the concrete wall, fly over the handlebars and pancake the concrete wall. My brother would skitter across the concrete and ask the most loaded question a brother can ask another brother: "Are you okay?" First not much movement, then as I imagine it, my hand begins to move, just a wiggle; I cough and dust from the concrete floor kicks up and settles. I slowly rise, epic music playing in the background, the total Jerry Bruckheimer shot. "Yes, yes, I am!" Then my brother would utter the words, the words that only a brother could say to someone he almost put in Special Ed for the rest of his life. "You wanna do it again?" There was no hesitation. There was no contemplation. "Yes... yes I do wanna do it again!"

It may not have been that epic; I'm pretty sure Jerry Bruckheimer was never in our basement, but to me, now, a man somewhere in his 40's, looking back at his childhood and his brother, my family amazes me. As I think back to my first memories of my childhood and the house that my parents built I wonder what are we building? Most of us are not going to build our own family house, hats off to you if you do. Things have changed: yes we wear seat belts, your kids are the weird ones if they are not wearing a helmet most of the time and Under Armor is the new Duke. But each one of

EVERYTHING ELSE

us as parents gets the opportunity to build. What stories are you building as a family? What memories are you building as a family? I think my dad is pretty amazing for building the house I grew up in and for working nights and weekends so we could have a roof over our heads. But that is not the most amazing thing that my dad built. I remember my dad playing catch with me; I remember watching Monday Night Football together and him eating sardines. He built me. He built who I am and he built a framework for who I want to become. I remember my dad loving my mom more than my brother and I and never envied her or harbored hatred for him. I knew that was a smart thing to do because someday, it would be the Big Wheel that was covered with dust and the basement would be quiet. He knew that when my we left, it was going to be just them. I remember my dad opening his Bible on Sunday mornings at the breakfast table and reading. I remember my dad walking through some of the most difficult times and always managing to put his family first. My dad built some amazing things, but none greater than his family.

What are you building? My parents sold that house several years ago, but the memories are still with us. No matter where we end up, we always call that house home, the house that my dad built so that he could build us. It was always home to the Laxtons. It will always be what we built as a family. And I'm pretty sure there's still some blood residue in the basement…

Big Brother

My brother, Mark (shaking my head as I think of him and smile.) Remember when I told you he was a great big brother? There is only one time I can remember him picking on me and now that I think about it, he was actually trying to offer me a warning, the kind that keeps a little brother alive despite his own bright ideas. We had a fireplace in our family home and Illinois winters can be really cold, so we made use of the fireplace… and who doesn't like to play with fire?

It's a big deal, when you are a little kid, to be trusted with grown-up things like riding in the front seat of the car or lighting the paper in the fireplace. This particular day it was my turn to spark up the home fire; my brother knew it and he wanted to light the fire. I was determined that I would not give up my match to my older brother just because he had told me to give up my match. Things like this have a way of working themselves out and this time it worked itself out like this: my brother had picked me up by the collar and

EVERYTHING ELSE

calmly reminded me, kind of like a Soprano, that it was his turn to light the fire, in case I had forgotten.

At this point, my dad showed up and my brother dropped me with immediacy. See, there was no fighting in our house… that was the rule. One time I told my brother I hated him, ONE time. Those words never passed through my lips again. That day, as Mark held me off the floor insisting that my turn was his turn, my dad told him to go ahead and do his worst to me, and then it would be Dad's turn to do his worst to Mark.

I knew he meant it. I knew it because when he had heard me tell Mark that I hated him he had not been in the room. But he soon showed up. He heard those words and before I knew it I was being carried down the hall. My dad was not a screamer, he never got really angry and he always chose his words very carefully. He didn't have much to say, but when he spoke, it was important enough that everything stopped, every voice quieted and every ear listened. My dad sat me down in my room and in a stern, caring voice explained that those words were to never come out of my mouth again. "When your mom and I are gone someday he is going to be the only family from this house left. He is your brother." With that memory his words are forever etched in my mind. My brother and I live 12 hours apart, but when we are reunited, we are those two people who can pick up right where they left off the last time they were together. It's like time never passes between us. My father taught us that we are important to each other and we should always make sure we remain important to each other. Right now, he is my only brother; someday he will be my only family.

EVERYTHING ELSE

Baseball, Slurpees and Death

I like to think of my childhood antics as if they are the stars in the sky. Not because they were so miraculous or breathtaking, but because God only knows how many there were. I was in trouble… most of the time… too many times to count, in fact. But Mark, well Mark got in trouble exactly three times. Mark was compliant. He would do what he was told. Once he had talked back and my parents told him to go wash his mouth out with soap and he did it… by himself. My parents didn't walk him to the bathroom; they didn't have to grab the soap. They didn't have to stick it in his mouth and wrestle around with him while they tried to count to 30. They told him to do it so he did. Who does that? My brother does. He still does.

One afternoon when I was in second grade my dad and I were in an empty lot playing catch. I was a pitcher on my baseball team and Dad assumed the catcher's position to work with me. Mark wandered over to us, bat in hand and Dad told him to stand in position to give me a strike zone. Mark, of course, complied. He walked up to the

EVERYTHING ELSE

make believe batter's box, put his bat up and got in the batting position. Dad dropped into the catcher's position and before I started my wind up looked up at Mark and delivered, what I now know to be one of the most important pieces of information that my brother would ever receive from my dad. "Mark," Dad said, dropping to the squat and staring up at my bat-wielding, totally compliant older brother. "Don't swing that bat." Dad didn't have a catcher's mask on. "If you foul one off it could hit me," Dad stressed, still looking at Mark. "I just want Brett to have a strike zone to look at."

Mark, who had been looking at my dad, nodded and turned his attention to me. I started my wind up. Left foot back, bringing my arms up, kicking the leg and exploding off of the pitching rubber... It was a beautiful pitch. It took a slight arch up, so quickly that you wouldn't see it if you didn't know how to look for it, then began a sweet slide, coming in right at Mark's knees. Perfection. From the mound, I watched it happen, completely helpless. I saw Mark's eyes grow big and he licked the corner of his mouth. He gently stepped into the perfect pitch, eyes glazed over as if being controlled by some unseen force of nature. He wanted a piece of that ball... Because it was so beautiful, because Dad had said no, because he was caught up in the glory that comes with a casual game of baseball; the world will never know. Mark swung a mighty bat, picking up speed ready to meet the ball in mid-flight.

If you speak baseball, you know that if a batter fouls a pitch straight back it is said, "the batter barely missed that pitch." On that day, in that empty lot, after being told specifically not to swing, my brother

barely missed that pitch and fouled it straight back into Dad's unprotected, completely exposed, unsuspecting nose. It was like someone has pressed the button on the Slurpee machine at a 7-11. Dad's nose exploded, a cannon of blood spewing out as he crumpled backward and did not move. I don't handle pressure well. I fold or at least that is what I want to do. That is what I did at this point; I collapsed on the pitcher's mound, certain that my brother, the compliant one, the good son had killed my dad.

Then I began to cry. "Oh great…" I sobbed. "You killed Dad! You killed Dad!" Mark stood there, bat in hand, looking back and forth from his allegedly dead father to his mentally crippled little brother. I can't imagine what Mark must have been thinking or feeling. On one side there's your poor little brother who may never pitch again due to the trauma and on the other, there's your father that you just bludgeoned with a ball hit by a bat that you were explicitly told to not swing.

Then, Dad moved. He rolled over in obvious pain. We weren't used to seeing that. Dad is a hard-working man with fingers that bear the scars of manual labor. He was the type of guy that would drill a hole in his hand to relieve the pressure of smashed, swelling fingers. The guy that carried a pocket knife just in case he needed to dig out a splinter or clean his teeth. Once, he cut off two of his fingers with a saw, sent a text to my mom to tell her he needed to go to the hospital and then fixed himself a glass of soda while he waited for her to get to the house. He is the Chuck Norris of the Midwest. He wasn't dead, but he was in pain. My dad got up, looked at my brother and in a very calm voice said, "Mark run home." When I say "calm voice" you need to imagine Liam Neeson in Taken meets Galdalf for a study date in the library: quietly, calmly with an edge of terrifying knowledge that someone has made a massive mistake. I wonder now, looking back, what the neighbors must have thought as they watched the events unfold: my brother running down the street crying, dragging his bat relieved because Dad was alive and terrified because of the exact same thing, and my bloodied, broken dad walking like an extra from the cast of Thriller. One hand on his face trying to stop the

EVERYTHING ELSE

blood Slurpee formerly known as his nose, his other hand holding mine, and me, a slobbering, snotty mess of tears and mud still wailing because my dad wasn't dead.

There are many reasons why that memory sticks with me, but mainly it sticks with me because that might be the first memory I have of truly understanding how much Dad loved us. I mean, we knew that our father loved us, but we also knew that we would get in trouble if we didn't follow his instructions. He loved first and spoke second, but was always teaching by his actions. He taught us that love means discipline, but it also means forgiveness. I never knew how much trouble Mark got into for that; I don't really know what happened the rest of that day, but I do know that my dad never allowed Mark to attend another one of our pitching sessions.

EVERYTHING ELSE

Manliness, a Ford & a Bully

It was the summer before my freshman year in high school; it was 1988… I remember growing up in the 70s and 80s; to say it out loud or see it on paper makes it feel so ancient. As I am writing this I am really beginning to grasp how long ago 1988 was…

I always flew under the radar, I didn't want to get singled out or picked on. I am not sure where this fear came from but I spent so much time fearing others that I allowed it to shape the kind of persona I portrayed. I was the nice guy, easy to get along with, never been in a fight in my life. Even to this day, the closest thing to a fight I have ever been a part of was when I punched a neighbor in the face… in third grade. I wish I could say he said something about my momma and so I laid him out, but I think we were in his backyard fighting over a ball. I punched him… and then I made a real statement about my manliness by running home and crying. At this point it would take approximately two purses and a bracelet to turn me into a full-fledged woman, I know, but it is totally true. I punched him, and then I ran home crying.

We had a town bully, Sam. I didn't know Sam. He went to another school and I had never met him, only heard rumors. One day I was standing in a parking lot with my baseball team getting ready to leave for an away game, when Matt Woodward delivered the news that would change the course of my summer. "Hey Brett, you know Sam?" Matt asked, toeing the concrete of the parking lot. Of course I knew who Sam was… "Well, Sam doesn't like you…"

How could this be? I had never even met Sam; how could he not like me? And if he ever met me, he would most certainly like me. I was funny. I was the nice guy. I was easy to get along with. I was green beans; I went great with anything. But as I stood there, stunned by Matt Woodward's news, I realized something. It didn't matter. I was on Sam's radar. I had seen Sam at the baseball fields and at the pool, but never, not once had I talked to him or made eye contact, nothing…but it changed my summer. I spent the rest of the summer being where Sam was not…and this worked out well until late in the summer when Sam found me.

I was in the locker room at the pool getting ready to go home. Sam walked in with one of my friends so I thought maybe the whole Sam Encounter wasn't going to end badly. I mean, I knew my friend would be there for me. Sam began to taunt me. He started splashing water from the sink at me and started calling me names and yet my friend did nothing. He wouldn't even look at me. He just stood there and I got the feeling that he was just waiting for the whole thing to be over with. I can't blame him though. I am not sure what I would have done either. We all like to think we would play the hero, but in the situation when the pressure is on and you are 14 years old, it easier to imagine being a hero than it is to actually be one. I ignored it all, thinking if I can ignore him, then he would go away. I was wrong.

EVERYTHING ELSE

I walked out and Sam followed me. My brother was supposed to pick me up from the pool but he wasn't there yet. Sam continued to call me names and push me and I finally realized that I had to do something. This wasn't going to go away. I couldn't hide under the blankets. I might have to punch someone again and this time if I landed the punch, I couldn't run away crying. Then there is always the haunting thought that lingers in the mind of every person who has ever been confronted with physical defense: this might be the last punch I throw before I die. So I turned around and for the first time in my life I made eye contact with Sam. Sam walked up to me and asked what I was staring at. There was no way I could talk…I was so scared that I felt my larynx taking a nosedive down into my stomach and I knew my puberty voice would totally wreak havoc on my first man moment. There I was nose to nose with the bully Sam… then I heard it.

It was beautiful, a mixture of smooth melodic gears and the hearty chug of pre-emission engines. I heard the sound of a Ford Granada. This is the very car that had taken us on countless vacations across the country, the same car with white vinyl interior, red on the outside and big all over. I can't say I ever remember having an emotional connection with a car, but this day, this beautiful beast of a vehicle was rounding the corner and piloting this chariot is the hero of this story.

Sam was in trouble, but he didn't know it yet. He didn't know that the sound approaching him from behind was the sound of my rescue and his demise. My brother pulled up to the curb with a screech. This would be one of two memories of my brother in the Granada; one was pleasant, the other not so much. This was the pleasant one. (The other one was when he dropped me off at junior high while he was arguing with his girlfriend. I had gotten out of the car and walked over to ask him a question. He was looking at his girlfriend and he ran over my toes. But that could be forgiven, easily, because Mark and the Granada had come to my rescue.)

I stood a little taller, something that happens as you let go of your fears. Mark got out of the car and told me to get in. And I did. I have no idea what Mark said to Sam, but Sam never picked on me again. It's funny how we run, run, run from things until we allow it to corner us, which it always does, usually when we least expect it. Whatever it is, whoever it is that has set us on the run, there will come a time when we will have to stop and face it or deal with the truth that we will die regretting not facing it. Such a double-edged sword.

It cannot be denied either that we are much braver when surrounded by others who share our mindset. Makes me wonder how people live without a community, without a church... Don't live alone, God created us for community. You never know when your "Sam" might have you cornered and you need the chariot and the person driving the chariot to tell you to get in the car because "they got this." I got in the car and my fear was gone. Amazing how just one person standing shoulder to shoulder with you can give you this courage, isn't it?

I look at life and how God has created us for each other. The strength, the courage, the laughter, the tears are better with each other. I wonder sometimes what people in our lives need to know that we are just around the corner. All of us have gotten that e-mail or text message, that tweet from someone that made our day, they made the clouds not so thick, they made the sun a little brighter, they made the rain something to play in instead of sitting inside. If those that are around us make us so much better, then who around you can YOU "make" better? Who can YOU encourage? Don't wait to send that text message; it will take a couple of minutes for you to make someone's day better. So I challenge you today to dust off the old Granada, whip

EVERYTHING ELSE

around a corner or two and screech to the rescue of someone who needs to know that you've got this.

EVERYTHING ELSE

EVERYTHING ELSE

Bath Time, Army Men, & the Family Bible

Things are better shared…aren't they? Ice cream is good, but ice cream with a friend is so much better. That same adage applies to getting into trouble as well. It's better, somehow, to get a beat down with a friend rather than alone, to have someone to feel your pain. Baths are better with someone else as well…

This would be one of those moments where you decide you're either on board with this book or you're going to gently lay it down and step away… Still here? Okay, let's clarify. I am not talking about with your wife or husband because life is not an episode of Days of Our Lives and that's a whole other book that I will never write. What I'm talking about is sibling soup… If you have a sibling anywhere near your age, then chances are you shared some bath time with them. As an adult, looking back on this phenomenon, I feel relatively disgusted. When I was young, pools of water were unspoken permission for pee-pee action. Now, looking back on this, I am hoping the same isn't true of my brother. Nonetheless, we shared some bath time together and during that bath time we shared army men. You remember these, the pre-posed green plastic men with a flat plate attached to their feet so they could stand? Mark had thousands, no lie. He used to spend hours setting up a battle in the basement, calculating every placement of every army man.

He would set up two different factions in a face off and then, he would roll a marble on behalf of one faction to knock down the lines of the opponent. If a man fell to the marble, it was Taps. Mark would switch from one side to the other and the army with the last man standing was the victor. Then he would set them all up and do it again. My brother is a patient man. I am not. I tried to play this game, but got bored. What the game needed was a giant (me) to stomp all of the men on both sides, leaving the giant (me) as the lone victor.

The army men were also part of bath time. For the life of me, I can't remember how we made them relevant within the boiling pot of our sibling soup, but what I do know is that army men in the bathtub sometimes lead to some very special maneuvers. In this particular instance, the army men were sent on a mission to find out approximately how many of their special forces could be packed into the bathtub faucet. It was a brief mission, though many were willing to sacrifice, because after my brother shoved a couple up in the faucet, he couldn't get them out. MAN DOWN!

We tried everything because, as anyone who ever played with army men knows, there is no man left behind, ever. Our fingers couldn't reach them and other toys didn't work. Then my brother who, if you remember, was much better than me when it came to dealing with highly intense situations came up with brilliant idea: turn the water on and allow the pressure to simply shoot them out. It didn't work. Water squirted everywhere like a thumb-covered garden hose.

EVERYTHING ELSE

It became clear that these men might not come back from this mission. I watched panic blossom across Mark's face as I dibbled and dabbled in the water. I wasn't nervous because I didn't do it. This was the rare .000001 percent of the time that the blame could not be placed on me and I took great pleasure in that moment.

My mother came in to check on us and soon our covert operation wasn't so covert. "There are army men stuck in the faucet?" She looked at us, two soggy noodle heads floating in our sibling soup. Then came the Commander-In-Chief. Certain to get to the bottom of the failed faucet mission, there were no bushes that were to be beaten. "Who put the army men in the faucet?" There are moments of joy that a man experiences throughout his life: seeing the birth of his first child, waking up in the middle of the night and finishing off the last piece of cheesecake, and any and every Myth Buster's episode. But none, none came close to the joy I felt as I sat there in the tub with my brother knowing that he would have to pony up and take responsibility. I was wearing the ultimate Colgate smile and if you listened closely enough, you could have heard the delicate "ting" of the sparkle coming off of my toothy grin. Again, the Commander-In-Chief questioned, "Who put the army men in the faucet?"

I was going to get to say that phrase that means so much to the younger brother who suffers from an overabundance of curiosity and mischief. Those two little words that trigger the angelic fanfare; I was going to say them. "Not me." It was time for Mark to pay the piper.

But before I could even get the tip of my innocent tongue to the top of my soft pallet, Mark looked at Dad and in my one moment of hesitation he took the words right out of my mouth... literally. "Not me..." He said. What? No? No! If we hadn't been sitting in the bathtub his pants would have burst into flames. I couldn't believe it! Honest Abe lied. I told my parents over and over again that I didn't do it, but I had a record, I had a mug shot, I'm pretty sure they were keeping a file on me, kind of like a police record but more like a profile. I was a serial offender. Mark was a good guy in a bad situation as far as they were concerned. They did what any loving, caring parents would do. They split us up and began the waterboarding.

They pulled the good cop/bad cop routine and I got the bad cop. Dad had it all over me. It wasn't going to take anything other than thinking back a couple of days to my last family felony... I was no patsy, though and I knew what was at stake. That night we were supposed to go roller-skating. In the 80s, going roller-skating was the equivalent to a trip to Europe today. The 80s were amazing like that: roller-skating, glam rock, and actually eating the food at Dairy Queen. Who does that now? I don't know anyone that actually eats there anymore, but the in the 80s we did and we roller-skated. We sometimes did them both in the same night.

Things had taken a turn for the worse in Interrogation Room 1 and I was preparing myself to ask for my token cigarette and cup of crappy coffee. My parents informed us that if someone didn't take responsibility for the crime, there would not be any roller-skating. I stayed strong assuring my dad that I did not do this horrible thing. With whispered conferences between the parents and the careless mention of the word "spank" it was heating up. My door was open and I saw my mom walking towards my brother's room with the family Bible.

I'm not sure why we called it that; it was huge and heavy and we never used it for any Bible times in our family, it was just a showpiece as far as I remember. But on this night when I saw my mom hauling this massive book down the hallway, I thought she was surely going to beat the

Word of God into my brother. No lie. I considered how humiliating that would be for Mark and how nearly physically impossible that might be for Mom. This was definitely a consideration that was irrational; my parents were kind and gentle and never beat us. But I had been on the inside for so long with the bad cop. I panicked, certain that our family Bible was going to become a weapon of mass instruction for my brother and possibly the cause of a very uncomfortable rotator cuff injury for my mother. It was in a moment of perverted nobility that I took the blame upon myself, certain that when I confessed my brother would see my courage and love for him and surely step in and save me, confessing to the whole thing. He did not.

The Laxtons did roller skate that night, only after I got spanked. I told my 10-year-old daughter about this story and she advised that I should continually remind her Uncle Mark of that sacrifice. I took her advice, so much so that I decided to write it down so he and his family for years to come would remember the great sacrifice that I endured that evening so my brother would not get beat with a Bible, my mother would not suffer a fantastically painful injury to her back or shoulder and so our family could spend the night stayin' alive at the roller rink. I think that is what families should do for one another. I hear about families and brothers who are at odds with each other, who haven't spoken for years and who harbor painful thoughts about favoritism or jealousy. I believe God created families to make us tougher, to make us a little more gentle and to show us that we need to rely on others at times. I feel blessed to know that even if the world goes away I still have my family who will stand by me. I believe that God created families to share dirty bath water, to make growing and living more fun… and yes, He created family to take the beatings for one another…. Mark, you owe me!

EVERYTHING ELSE

EVERYTHING ELSE

Vampires, Snapping Turtles & a BB Gun

When you are young, your dad is omniscient. He is, in essence, your very own encyclopedia, or to the modern youngster, Google in a book. My dad had to have known everything: he built our house, he drew up the blue prints, he fixed our cars, our bikes, our scratches and even knew how to cook, as long as it was on the grill. When I was little I had a Red Rider BB gun that had zero power. To hit something you had to play the angle of the BB dropping because it had very little velocity. I took my BB gun and would shoot at trees or the mailbox most of the time. Every once in a while, a frog with incredibly bad timing would hop by and become a victim of the right angle and bad velocity. I would have to shoot the frog seven or eight times just to slow it down and most of them probably died, not from the BB actually penetrating an organ, but from boredom. If the BB

EVERYTHING ELSE

didn't kill it, I would eventually take mercy on the frog and smash it with a rock.

One time I was down in our woods and came across a huge black snake on a tree. I unloaded on it. I lost count of how many BB's I shot it with and when I carried it back to my house on a stick it was still wriggling and winding, but it did however have some pretty serious BB indentions all over its head. I knew that my father would be proud. We were not hunters, but I knew that showing him how I had taken down this Goliath of a snake would impress him. He did not disappoint. When I took it to him he showed me the real magic. He chopped off its head and skinned the snake like it was something he did daily. Then he took the body and dropped it into the bucket of cold water and it began to twirl in the bucket. I was amazed. All I could wrap my mind around was the fact that my dad was the coolest. And I was a little nervous that he knew how to do that to a snake. It's not in any of the encyclopedias; knowledge of this level came only from years and years of trying weird and crazy things. As a child, Dad once tied two cats together by the tails with string and then hung them over a clothesline to watch them fight. When my grandmother saw the flurry of fur and teeth dangling from her clothesline, she made Dad stick his hand in the middle of the two fighting cats and untie them. He said it left him with more scratches than he could count. How did he even know how to do that? I would have never of thought of such a genius idea.

In the home that my father built for our family, we had a fireplace, a real one, with real wood that you had to split, with real fire and real smoke. Not like these electric fireplaces with lights to make it look like a fire. It was the read deal. I remember one night while our family was in the living room, probably playing our Atari (another 80s phenom), something made a noise in the fireplace. My dad went over and opened the glass doors to the fireplace and found nothing. He looked up the chimney;

still nothing. It was that moment, the same moment when everything gets quiet in the really scary movie and all of the people just look at each other waiting for whatever "it" is that is going to happen, actually happens. Then it happened. What I assumed was a black bird came swooping out of the chimney into our living room. It scared the junk out of us; this bird flying through our living room running into the walls.

That's when I heard my dad say to my mother: "It's a bat." As a child you know two types of bats: the first is the bat you take to the empty lot to tip off a foul and bludgeon your father with; the second is the kind that bites you, sucks your blood and turns you into a vampire. The kind of bats that are fearless because once they have blood all they want is more blood and once you get what you really crave you become stupid with bravery. I had watched Scooby Doo; I knew this to be true. Without hesitation, my dad grabbed a blanket and began to chase the bat that, because he had not drawn fresh blood from my alluring, and I'm sure incredibly tasty throat vein, was still relatively intelligent and he kept eluding my dad. Finally, one last time, he threw the blanket and it landed right on top of that vampire bat. Dad grabbed the blanket and threw it outside saving us all from becoming the baseball-playing, roller-skating Count Dracula's it had intended.

My dad's affinity for all things nature-icky didn't end there. Once we were all watching Pee Wee's Big Adventure (quality 80s movie) and Dad called us outside. In our front yard was a huge alligator snapping turtle. He used a broomstick and showed us how you can't flip them over and how they can stick their heads way out to snap. He once brought home an injured duck and to this day I have no idea where he got it. He built a pen for it in the back and he nursed it back to health. We named him Donald because we were creative like

EVERYTHING ELSE

that. We took the duck to the lake near our house one day and set him free. Now I am 39 years old and I still have no idea how my dad knows all that he does. He can tell you the migrating habits of the humpback whale and reupholster your living room couch. Now, he does woodworking making beautiful furniture. He once made a bumper for an old truck we had. Where did he learn this?

    I know all that I know now because of my dad; but my grandfather (my dad's dad) was not around so I wonder where he picked up some of his knowledge. And when I look back, I can see that the coin was in the air sometimes in that some things worked out (like our house) and some things didn't (like the time he jumped from his roof with a sheet thinking it would act as a parachute). My dad wasn't afraid to make mistakes and I sometimes wonder if he was ever afraid of anything. It inspires me as a dad to learn, to make mistakes, to not be afraid. There are so many things I want to show my own kids, but the main thing I want to show them is that mistakes are nothing to be afraid of. In fact, they are usually the biggest indicator of growth. I read the following somewhere once and it really stuck with me: *don't be afraid to make mistakes, just make new ones*. I don't think I will ever know all that my dad knows, but I know that our children, mine and yours, are constantly looking for answers and I am not sure that I will know all the answers to the questions. But if I don't I will just ask my dad then tell my kids, and let them think that I know everything like my dad did. And I hope, someday, they will see me like I saw my dad: a blanket-wielding superhero who saved me from the Dracula bat.

EVERYTHING ELSE

Santa Claus, Christmas Ninjas, & Grandma Sleeping

My brother and I each had our own room, but from time to time, we would have a down-the-hall sleepover. We would stay awake and talk about the deep meaning of life. These talks were so deep and meaningful that I can actually only remember two of them. The first was when Mark broke the news to me about my parents' nocturnal activities. "They still do the thing to make babies, even though they are not going to make any more babies," Mark whispered in the darkness and I remember feeling the bottom drop out of my stomach. I stared at the ceiling, swallowing hard and being totally disgusted by that thought. Mom? Sweet, gentle Mom? And Dad? Why? There were so many other things they could do with their time… roller-skating, baseball, Atari!

That is an image that no child should ever have stuck in his head, and the problem is that once introduced, it sticks around forever! It was almost as traumatic as the other late-night revelation delivered to me by my big brother. He told me the truth about Christmas. He revealed that there was no North Pole and that the presents didn't come from where I had been told they come from. He also told me that he could prove it. Christmas was traditionally a down-the-hall sleepover night and so, a plan began to evolve, growing almost as if it had a life, a will and determination of its own. Mark revealed that it was actually Mom and Dad who put the presents under the tree and if we stayed awake long enough, we wait until they put the presents out, snag a preview of the untold joy to come, and be back in bed before the morning and no one would be the wiser.

    Like any danger-laced endeavor, we knew there would be obstacles and the biggest obstacle would be Grandma Laxton, who spent the night with us every Christmas eve and always slept on the couch in the living room. We were going to steal past Grandma without being discovered. With the news of Santa fresh on my mind, and a waning hope that Mark was mistaken, because who wants to believe that Santa doesn't really exist, we began the mission of sneaking down the hall to the living room. I was still not totally convinced about "Santa Gate", and in my mind sneaking down the hall to nail your parents playing Santa would definitely put me on the naughty list. So not being caught by my parents, and even more importantly, not being caught by Santa just in case my brother was wrong, shared equal space in my brain as we steeled ourselves for our mission. I was nervous, but I held on to the optimism that only a little brother being led on a super dangerous secret mission by his big brother could comprehend. We were in full Ninja mode, pressed against the hallways, hiding in the shadows. We were slowly achieving award winning Ninja status as we crossed and weaved, crossed and weaved down

EVERYTHING ELSE

the hallway. We made it into the living room and sure enough, set right in front of the fireplace were the gifts just like Mark had said. Mark's gifts were always wrapped in green wrapping paper and mine in red and this Christmas was no different. My brother was a genius! Not only had he figured out the Christmas secret, but he had led us to the pinnacle of brotherly mischief achievement: we were about to see our gifts before morning.

The last hurdle, the only thing standing between us and the legendary achievement was the sleeping outline of Grandma Laxton. But we were glory hungry now… we were Vikings in the prow of the ship raising our swords not only as a warning to the dragons, but also as an invitation. We began the final journey. In the back of my head, I was still scared and relatively certain we were breaking some cosmic Christmas law. Then it occurred to me that there was another law we might be breaking: God's law. I had this fear that God knew what we were doing and He was not at all happy about what was going down. Even if Santa wasn't real, I knew God was and He saw everything and He was especially aware of little boys that were being naughty. I figured naughty boys were high on God's priority list, right under serial killers, the cold war and disco. He was immune to being impressed by our Ninja stealth tactics. He was up there, watching this all go down… probably moving us up a notch or two on the priority list; we may even have surpassed disco.

But still we pressed on, dropping to the floor to complete the last jog of our journey. We were crawling next to my grandmother when it happened. Grandma was prone to night terrors. There are many scary things in life, but few are scarier than when an old woman is moaning or screaming in your ear as you crouch at ear level beside the couch on which she is sleeping. We eked forward; she began to moan. We took an itty-bitty baby scoot; she moaned and I stand by my word to this day that she whispered the words "no, no." She was in a deep

EVERYTHING ELSE

sleep in the middle of a night terror. I was absolutely and irrefutably convinced this was a sign from the Almighty God was speaking a warning through my grandmother and He was not happy.

I bolted. Mission aborted, every man for himself, and all the rules of Ninja craftiness out the window. It was just a race to get back in bed, under the covers and hope that the wrath of God had been appeased by the major cardiopulmonary event He had just caused two boys on that sweet holy night. I believe we found the courage to sneak back out that night and we did get a peak at Christmas. I am not sure if God was mad at us or not that night, but He may have been a bit more forgiving considering the good laugh I am positive we gave Him.

I think God has a sense of humor; if you doubt it, take a really good look at the duck-billed platypus. And in that same vein, I think that's why God made brothers and sisters We need our brothers and sisters to explain the things that we would never believe if they came from someone else. Mark was my brother. I knew he loved me. I knew I trusted him. Why would he lie to me about Santa? I still call my brother from time to time when I have heavy or big decisions to make because he is good like that; he will tell me the truth. He sees through the decorations, the wrappings, the glitter of lights and shiny things and sees the truth of whatever he is observing. I trust him, as I should, to tell me the truth no matter how harsh it may be, no matter how much it may hurt. I trust him to guide me, although I could have gone my whole life without knowing my parents had sex.

EVERYTHING ELSE

Bathroom Breaks, Screaming & Slapping Dad

It was another down-the-hall sleepover night and we were sound asleep when we were awakened by the sound of something falling with a thud to the floor. Actually it was more that I was awakened; Mark loved sleep so much that a flatbed truck full of dynamite would not have even touched his slumber. Then I heard my mother's voice rise in a scream. It was the same feeling that I get now as a father when I hear one of my children call out in the middle of the night; it is heart stopping. My mother screaming in the middle of the night was not normal and coupled with the sound of something hitting the floor was enough to make a person wet the bed, which I did on a regular occasion, but that's another book…

My parents had their own bathroom but for whatever reason this night when my dad got up to use the bathroom, he used the hallway bathroom. I could see that the bathroom light was on and I made my way out to the hallway the sound of my mother's screams still

EVERYTHING ELSE

bouncing off of the walls and back to my head. When I turned the corner, I saw my dad lying on the bathroom floor on his back and my mother on top of him screaming.

I'm going to stop for a minute and just let you know that Dad didn't have a heart attack or anything serious like that, because you looked a little tense and definitely worried. My dad, in fact, was fine. I tell you that because I want you to be able to understand the humor in the situation, so just take a deep breath.

Dad had passed out in the bathroom. There's never a good time to go all unconscious, but to do it in the middle of the night in the middle of the bathroom just adds insult to injury. I mean, you've already been tapped on the shoulder in the middle of the night by nature's call and you have probably spent anywhere from ten to fifteen minutes thinking it will go away, dreading having to get out of your warm bed and walk across the cold floor and then finally giving in and with every step vowing to quit drinking so much soda before you go to bed. So there he was, in the middle of the bathroom floor, my dad passed out cold and looking so peaceful and restful, like he was really having a good sleep. And I am sure he would have been if it hadn't been for the fact that my mother was sitting astride him on the bathroom floor repeatedly slapping him as she would chant "Dick, wake up! Wake up, Dick!"

I obviously get my coping skills from my mother. She handles pressure about as well as an egg in a microwave. Obviously, the first thought in my head is doing whatever I can to escalate the situation to full-on crisis mode. I took off down the hallway at full speed screaming, "My daddy is dead. My daddy is dead." It's at this point that my father wakes up to his sweet wife sitting on him like a jockey on Sea Biscuit, slapping him while she screams his name all played to the tune of his seven-year-old son running through the halls screaming about his daddy being dead.

EVERYTHING ELSE

If you've ever passed out and then come to, you know that you don't remember anything about the physiology of the fainting. The last thing you remember is the last thing you spend a good amount of time doing. In this case, my father thinks he has awoken to a woman gone mad.

"What are you doing?" he asks, rousing to a fully shocked expression. My mother, still frantic, tries to explain that he had passed out. Not recognizing that he was still in the bathroom he tried to convince my mother that he was just sleeping. Eventually everyone made his or her way back to bed, but I don't know if anyone slept that night... with the exception of Mark, my brother, who slept through the whole thing.

My dad lost that time. My brother slept through that memory. My mother and I remember it vividly. As a father now to a 10 year old and an 8 year old, I realize how quickly it all flies by, how as they grow older, time grows shorter. It becomes more and more of a reality every day that if we are not careful, these years will go by so fast and we will miss it. We will lose that time. We "sleep" through it, and by sleep, I mean we unintentionally detach ourselves from what is happening right now. Maybe for you, sleep is chasing a career, a promotion and better pay.

Maybe it's chasing the dream of your child being all-pro in whatever they participate in. My kids are involved in sports and chorus and drama and other activities for the right reasons, because they love them, but any number of parents are desperately, vicariously living through their children and not realizing that the chances of them becoming an international legend or even getting to play or participate for scholarship money someday are approximate to winning the lottery while being struck by lightning. These things are not bad in and of themselves; they can be a great way to connect with our kids. My son, Graham, is a pretty good shortstop and I love

EVERYTHING ELSE

watching his every at-bat in little league, but what I really want him to know is that being kind is more important to me. My daughter is one of the most creative kids I know. She creates some beautiful things, but what I really want her to know is that God created beautiful. For my wife and I to teach these things, we have to be intentional. We have to make sure we are "awake" at all times. We have to make sure we are chasing after the right things. If we are not careful our kids' will graduate, go to college, get married, have their own kids, and we will look back and realize we slept through the memory making.

EVERYTHING ELSE

Mrs. Newton, Street Smarts & Mini-Mart

Second grade for me was a year of firsts, a year of trying things out. There were the two times that my friend Billy and I missed the bus on purpose and decided that we would walk home. From the school to my home was around fifteen miles, literally all uphill. Billy lived around six miles away so we walked to Billy's and called my mom. The first time it happened, I didn't get in trouble. The second time Billy and I were walking next to a main road and someone recognized us and called my mother. I got in quite a bit of trouble that time.

Second grade was the first time I ever saw a woman chew tobacco. It was Billy's mother and yes, I have seen more than one girl chew; the second time was at the college softball world series. In second grade, I rode the bus, and in that hour on the bus I learned many of life's lessons. I learned what the birds and bees were all about and then some. I knew more than any second grader should know. There really should be some kind of legislation put into place to help protect the oblivious second graders from the vivid, albeit twisted information delivered about relationships by junior high school students.

The school bus is where I found one of my first crushes. She was in high school and dated one of the star athletes at our school. This same guy went on to play for the Cardinals and A's in the major leagues. She sat next to me sometimes because she thought I was cute; and by cute, I now realize that she saw me as a little brother type. Back then, it was true love and all I knew was that I made her laugh and she made me feel funny on the inside. One day she got on the bus and she was not wearing her boyfriend's class ring, an amazingly huge piece of metal that was sized down to her finger using yarn and bright-colored nail polish. So when the Empire State buildings of class rings went missing from her finger, it was noticeably absent. I asked her where it went and she explained that she and her boyfriend had broken up. I could only assume that she had realized that the boy on the bus was the man for her and she had broken off the pointless romance with a future multi-million dollar athlete to focus her attentions on the funny little boy on the bus. It seemed totally reasonable. I don't think we talked much after second grade, but she probably lays awake at night thinking about the one that got away. (Just so you know... I am the one that got away.)

In second grade I had a friend named Jimmy and Jimmy came to school every day with extra money. I am not sure if he was supposed to buy extra milk with it or what, but he didn't. Jimmy and I used that money for a loftier purpose. We would sneak off school grounds, which sounds more devious than it really is because all we truly did was just walk out of school. If that happened today, can you imagine the lawsuits and suspensions? We had around ten minutes to kill before we had to be back in the building so we would sprint up one block to main street and over two blocks to the mecca of all stores: The Mini-Mart.

At the Mini-Mart an enterprising young man could purchase soda, newspapers, some groceries, baseball cards, cigarettes (that came later in my rebellious years), and candy. The Mini-Mart always had the newest and best candy, but I was a man of habit, always going for the sucker that doubled as a whistle. We would spend Jimmy's money and then sprint back to the building just in time for class to start while still picking the hard sucker out of my teeth. I never had time to really enjoy the candy, just bite down into and scarf it down because there was no way that a treat like that would wait until lunch. We were candy runners, living on the edge and our second grade teacher, Mrs. Newton, had no idea what we were doing. See, I was a little smarter than the other kids. I wasn't necessarily report card smart, but I was street smart. I could work an angle, find the loopholes and halo my way out of just about anything. I was the type of smart that comes from long bus rides with talkative older kids, the type of smart you get from cornfield running, the type of smart that is caught, not taught. I was a grade school gangster. Not the type of gangster with their pants around their knees and a tow chain hanging from their neck, I was the slick, sweet-talking, white-tooth smile Rat Pack gangster… a smooth criminal.

When we would first arrive in Mrs. Newton's class she would take the lunch orders and call roll to see who was there and who was not. During these ten minutes or so she needed her second grade class to keep busy as to not disrupt the crazy accounting skills it took to count heads, see who was having hot lunch and assess the current white vs. chocolate milk demographic split. During this time she gave morning worksheets. They were just math problems like: Johnny has three apples, he gives away one apple to Mary and gives

EVERYTHING ELSE

another half to Jimmy. So how many miles did Johnny have to walk to burn off 700 calories that day? This is what math looked like to me, impossible and irrelevant questions. We didn't even have a Johnny or Mary in our class.

When the work was completed it went into a tray on her desk. If you did not complete the work it would be saved to be completed when you had nothing to do or when Mrs. Newton was feeling particularly witchy. It was my keen smooth criminal skills that brought about an observation one day. At the end of the day, Mrs. Newton would take the sheets out of the tray and throw them away. She didn't even grade them! She didn't look at the names, nothing! This was busy work, work designed just to keep us busy, and in my mind, busy work was wrong! So I decided to try something one day.

I didn't turn in my work… the minutes passed by turning into hours, stretching into recess, then lunch, then second recess then the last bell. School was over and she didn't even know that I had not turned it in nor did she care. That was the day I figured out I was smarter than the average second grader. I stopped doing the morning work and I saved my sucker from the Mini-Mart. While other kids slaved away at the worthless work counting apples for Johnny, I would lift up my desktop, stick my head in and take a lick, then put the top back down as to not draw attention. This went on for some time, every day the same. But there was a fatal flaw in my seemingly perfect plan: the evidence. The blank worksheets from each day, the ones I wasn't doing were being stuffed haphazardly under the books in my desk.

Well as you can imagine the evidence began to stack up and soon I was left with a large mound of paper sticking out from underneath my desk. I could barely get the lid on my desk closed. Then it happened. One afternoon after the second recess, I sat there at my desk. I just sat. And Mrs. Newton came walking by and asked me

EVERYTHING ELSE

if I didn't have anything to work on. She was on to me, she had the goods, but I could still play it off. Smooth criminal. Smooth criminal. Smooth criminal... I looked up at her, halo shimmering and answered with a confident, "Nope!"

She didn't buy it. She reached for the lid of my desk, lifted it and began to take out books that were filled with or hiding unfinished papers. The papers flew everywhere; they came out of the middle of books, from under the books, dropped like little telltale rats from my desk. Right there in the middle of class she pulled out every paper, unpacking all of my street smarts, stacking them in a pile and telling the world that while yes, I was a criminal, I was most definitely not a smooth one. When she finally stopped, the evidence was overwhelming; this case was a slam-dunk for the prosecution. She stapled them together and handed out her punishment. She was judge, jury and in this case, executioner; she threw the book at me, the maximum sentence allowed for a case like this.

"You will finish all of these papers." She handed me the thick stack from behind her desk and I kept it low-key. So far so good, this was to be expected. It wouldn't be fun, but I could finish these. But for Mrs. Newton, a life sentence wasn't enough. She wanted more than blood. She wanted an example, a cautionary tale, a living, breathing warning. "Have your parents sign the top sheet," and in the back of my mind, I heard the steel-barred door slide, slam and latch. Life was over; it was all I could do not to lose it right there in front of my class. Smooth criminal... smooth criminal... I had to hold it together. I couldn't let my class see me cry. They had already seen me pee my pants in this very classroom.

We had been in the middle of some standardized testing, serious tests, no bathroom breaks, no water, no food, no talking, no fun, no joy. Just a paper book, a bubble sheet for answers and two No. 2 lead pencils plus the warning she had issued at the beginning of the test: "Go to the bathroom now, because once we start there are no breaks!"

I didn't have to go at that time; I'm pretty sure I stayed in the room and ate a sucker or something. But 15 minutes into a 90-minute session, my pea-sized bladder was waking up to say hello! I made it through the entire session and at the clock strike of the ninety-first minute, in the time that it took me to walk to her desk to ask if I could go to the bathroom, my pea-sized bladder betrayed me.

"Can I...?" and then my body answered in the form of a pizza-sized puddle that I created in front of her desk. A pea-sized bladder can hold a lot of ... pee. What do you do at that point? No one pulls you aside and tells you how to react when you pee your pants in front of all of your cronies. And evidently street smarts end at the corner of Bladder St. and Control Blvd. when it comes to peeing your pants. Billy Madison had not yet made peeing your pants cool. I had also chosen that day to wear my nearly new parachute pants that, true to the name, were made out of nylon silk much like parachutes. The nylon and the urine joined forces to create what can only be called a horrific, urine-laced shrink-wrap, creating a vacuum of sorts and sucking on to my legs. I looked like I was wearing black saran wrap.

So to maintain some semblance of the street-wise, dapper gangster my class had come to count on, I had to not cry. I couldn't cry and pee my pants in the same year. On the bus ride home that night, I thought about how much I enjoyed my life, how much I enjoyed food, sunlight, my friends, and how all of that was coming to an end for me. My parents were not going to take well to this latest development. I was hoping for an out-date of 20 years max... I had almost resigned myself to the fatality of the entire scenario when I suddenly remembered who I was. I was a smooth criminal. The paper would be signed, the work would be done and the whole thing would be over without my parents actually knowing that the incident had ever gone down. I was going to start a prolific career in forgery.

I was going to sign my dad's name to the paper. I chose my dad's name to forge because my dad's handwriting was almost worse than mine. The only issue I had to overcome was that I knew to sign an important document like this it had to be done in cursive and I had not learned cursive yet. Cursive did not come along with my street smarts training. I had to find something that had my dad's signature so that I could lay the sheet on top of his signature and trace it.

I found a document. It was sitting on top of our TV. We had a tradition that on birthdays, Valentines Day and other special card-giving events my mother would display the cards on top of the TV for the viewing pleasure of others. It was February and there was a fresh, new card on top of the TV sporting my dad's official signature. I snagged the card, took it to my room, laid the sheet on top of the card and with a sharp No. 2 lead pencil traced his signature. It went relatively well; there were several erase marks, one that smeared pretty badly instead of erasing, but I was going to give myself an "A" for effort. I put the card back and that night completed every sheet.

The next day I took that stack of papers and walked to Mrs. Newton's desk. I was confident, because confidence was key; teachers can smell fear. I took the stack with my dad's signature on the cover sheet and I laid it on Mrs. Newton's desk. She looked at it, then looked at me, then looked at it again. She was really inspecting it and it was with the second glance from her that I knew things were not going well, that she might suspect my forgery. She looked at me. Smooth criminal. Smooth criminal. Smooth criminal. "Brett, did your dad really sign this?" her voice was soft, almost as she felt sorry for me. I read it as embarrassment at her ability to question my exquisite first try at forgery. I looked right back at her and realized that I felt sorry for Mrs. Newton. That she wasn't like me. That she would never

EVERYTHING ELSE

understand the level of intelligence at which street smart people like myself operate.

"Yep!" I answered enthusiastically.

That was the day that I met Mr. McDonald, our elementary school principal. The document that I used to copy my father's formal signature was a Valentine's Day card from a husband to his wife, so the signature that Mrs. Newton saw that day that was supposed to be from the dad of a child that was in trouble to a teacher read: *Love, Dick*. The jig was up.

I got in quite a bit of trouble. My dad pulled up from work that day and my mom was sitting on the porch crying, because she was worried that her baby was going to grow up to be a hardened criminal, traveling the country living on checks forged with the diabolical signature: Love, Dick. I found out some years later that when my mom told my dad what I did, he couldn't hold back the tears of laughter. He thought it was the funniest thing that his son would hand a teacher a signature like that. Mind you, when he came into my room that evening he wasn't laughing, and I didn't laugh either. I decided after that day that trying to be a smooth criminal was actually kind of rough and I should give up the street smarts thing. But Jimmy and I still made a Mini-Mart run almost every day and we never got caught

EVERYTHING ELSE

A Box, Secrets & Moonings

My neighborhood running crew consisted of all boys and one girl. Many of the boys in the neighborhood were much older than I was and most of them were a couple of years older than my brother, making them anywhere from six to eight years older than me. They let me hang out with them most of the time because I didn't get on their nerves and I was a walking, talking, instant feedback focus group for their science experiments. I was also small enough that I came in handy when they needed a small checker-out-er or a retriever. I could fit just about anywhere. In third grade, we would play what I assumed was hide and seek, but considering the other boys were in high school, I'm pretty sure I was simplifying. What the game really turned into was "Hide Brett Where He'll Never Be Found." During one session, Bobby, the oldest of the crew, stuffed me into a dirty laundry hamper full of dirty laundry. It smelled terrible. He picked me up, placed me in, shut the lid, put the hamper in a closet, slid it under a shelf and closed the door. So there I was, in the dark closet at a neighbors house, packed in like a sardine in a basket full of laundry that smelled almost as terrible as sardines. I lasted a couple of minutes as I could hear the rest of the guys looking for me and it was fun being the object of a search party.

But then it got quiet and I started getting nervous. I wanted out. I pushed up to open the lid, but because the hamper had been hidden under a shelf the lid hit the bottom of the shelf and wouldn't open. I tried to remain calm, the operative word being "tried." We all know my history in pressure situations. Panic set in and I began to yell for help. Yelling turned into screaming and that quickly deteriorated into crying. I think what happened was that they looked for a while, Bobby told them where I was and they decided to take the game a bit further by waiting it out to see how long I could last. Eventually they came in and rescued me, all the while praising me for being so awesome and brave. Although I never played hide and seek with them ever again. I did pass this game on to a younger generation. We played with my friend's little brother one time and I hid him inside my bass drum on the drum set I had in the basement. I didn't, however, leave him in there long enough to panic or cause permanent damage to his respiratory system.

Every once in a while, the older boys would camp out in the woods next to Danny's house. Danny was one of the older boys and I was included in these campouts that taught me valuable skills. We got to go on missions late at night where we would stuff corn into mailboxes and set off fireworks on peoples' porches. These paled in comparison to the most important mission of all: the late-night mooning of passing cars. We would watch for headlights coming down the road and then all seven or eight of us would line up across the road. When the unsuspecting cars would round the corner about

EVERYTHING ELSE

100 yards down the road they would see seven or eight totally bare butts lined up across the road before we would pull up our pants and dash into the cornfields. It never occurred to me that we could be run over if one of us tripped or hit by a drunk driver... I thought this game was one of the best ever.

There is one adventure with my older mentors that will forever be burnt into my memory: the day we found the box. When you are young and you find a box it is like a treasure; your imagination runs wild thinking of the things that could be in that box: money, gold, fireworks or in this case, old magazines. I was in third grade and the older kids were talking about a box they found that was full of old magazines, old Playboy magazines to be specific. I didn't know what a Playboy was; my father never had these magazines in our house. The only magazines I can ever remember my dad owning were Popular Mechanics.

I followed the older boys into the woods to the place they had hidden this box. They promised me that this box held something so much better than anything you could find in a treasure map. I was so excited to see what was in this box- this box that was so important they had to hide it so no one else would steal the treasure. They opened the box and each boy pulled out a magazine. They didn't let me take one and I was sure it was because those magazines were so valuable and worth so much money they were afraid I would ruin them. I sat next to one of the boys and as he started to flip through these pages I realized that these boys weren't protecting a treasure, they were hiding a secret. Right there, in full color, were naked women. I had never seen a naked woman before and what began to pump through my heart was fear, disgust and excitement. I knew what I was looking at was wrong, but something in me would not allow me to look away. I am not sure how long we looked at them, but when we were finished looking through these magazines the boys told me over

EVERYTHING ELSE

and over that I must tell no one about what I had just seen. This was a non-issue for me. How do you tell your parents about what you've just seen when YOU have no idea what it is you've just seen that has already taken a foothold in your heart? I didn't tell anyone. But I kept going back. Something kept pulling me back when I was alone to that treasure chest to look at the images that had made me feel so excitingly disgusted and I went back regularly until the box disappeared.

But what didn't disappear was the thing that had been opened inside of me. The "treasure" opened up a Pandora's box in my life. It is something that grabbed that third grade boy and held on to this day.

As I got older, I found other magazines in neighbors' homes or in advertisements that started coming in the mail. One day, a videocassette showed up in our mailbox. We had a brand new VCR and one day with no one else at home I pulled out the VCR tape: a tape I had hidden so that no one would know that I had it. On that tape were people having sex. I had only seen still images so this was a whole new layer inside the Pandora's box. I found myself unable to turn away. After a few minutes of watching, I took the tape out and hid it in our backyard. One day, when Dad was mowing the grass, he found the tape. I ran to my room, sure that my dad would think it was me that had received this tape and then hidden it. I heard the slam of the door as my dad entered the house and I heard the white noise of snow as he turned on the TV. I heard the top of the VCR pop open and the plastic grating against plastic that meant the tape was going in. And then I heard the telltale sign that I knew so well, the dead giveaway that he had pushed play: the sound of men and women panting.

The video only played for a few seconds, and then I heard the pop of the tape being ejected. I stayed in my room, hoping my dad would not confront me. I am guessing that my dad threw it away because I never saw that tape again and my dad never said anything about it. I don't know if he ever said anything to Mark or not, but he kept my secret although he may not have ever known it was my secret to be kept.

In the years that followed I started actively looking for these images and tapes. Pornography grabbed me and held on for the next eight years. I kept thinking these desires would go away and that when I got into high school it would stop. It didn't. Certainly when I got to college, a Christian college, it would stop, but it didn't. I convinced myself that when I got married it would stop, but shamefully enough, it still didn't. The Internet was born and what I once had to search out was now at my fingertips. During my first year of marriage, I confided in a friend about my addiction and he suggested that I come clean to Amy and tell her everything. I sat Amy down one night and through tears told her the whole story and how I had been looking at these images on the Internet now, in our home, in the home we were building together. She cried. She was hurt. I didn't understand why. For me, it was nothing personal. It was just images on a screen that I needed, that fed a part of me that was so dark I had never been able to confess it before.

I understand now the hurt that I caused. In her mind, there was no way she could compete with these air-brushed and surgically-enhanced women whose only truly redeeming quality was their constant and enthusiastic compliance. What I was doing was cheating. And I would love to say that things have been perfect in our home since my confession and our resolve to get through it together, but they have not. The difference now for me is the relationships I have with people that I can be totally honest with. I have male friends that are committed to me in such a way that I can tell them anything. I can tell them my deepest secrets and they will not run. They are not just committed to me, but to my marriage and my family: and it has made all the difference.

Now that I have a son, I want to make sure I do all I can to protect him. I want to teach him that someday, as a man, he is going to have sexual desires, but that those desires cannot be handled outside the confines of marriage. Marriage is a commitment and protection for us. God created sex and sex is a powerful thing. It has the power to create life; but it also has the power to absorb it. The power of sexual activity that is found outside of marriage has the ability to cripple what God has created us to be. I want to make sure that Graham feels comfortable talking to me about anything and that shame is an awful thing. Shame keeps secrets. It keeps things in the dark and things in the dark get rotten and moldy and can only be destroyed when brought to the light.

And then there is my sweet, beautiful daughter, whom I try to convince on a daily basis that boys are smelly and gross. I warn my son not to be seduced by the lure of sexuality, by girls who will use their looks and their demeanor to ensnare him. I want to protect Tyler, my daughter, from boys that have already been seduced by that lure, that only have one thing on their minds. I know that there are going to be awkward conversations coming my way with Graham. One of my friends who has four sons told me not too long ago that he had his first sex talk with his oldest son. He said his son just stared at him with a look of complete disgust:

"You do THAT with mom?!"

Another one of my friends said that after he had told his son about sex he asked him if he had any questions. His son replied no, but as he started to walk out of the room his son spoke up:

"Hey dad, when I am married, do I HAVE to do that?!" Crazy how that will all change in a few short years, right? But as parents, we are called to protect, to make sure that the Internet is monitored in our

EVERYTHING ELSE

homes, to put the family computer in an open place and not to trust our kids so much. I hear parents talking about how you have to trust your children and yes, there is a place for trust, but we would never trust our kids to play with something that is dangerous, something that could injure or hurt them or even worse, hurt their hearts. Pornography and other perversions of beauty are just as dangerous to our children by encouraging them to start keeping secrets and living in shame. We have to talk; even when that conversation might be uncomfortable for everyone involved, ESPECIALLY when that conversation might be uncomfortable for everyone involved. If you aren't giving them the information as a parent, they will find it somewhere else. I am going to protect Graham physically, mentally, emotionally and sexually. I can't be everywhere with him, but I am going to do all that I can to make sure I do everything in my power to protect him when I can and in my home. And I promise Graham will not be going on any treasure hunts with older boys.

EVERYTHING ELSE

High School BFFs

I need to introduce you to Brett. Not me Brett, Brett the other Brett. Yes, I have a best friend with the exact first name as myself. I was in Junior High when I first met Brett. I was sitting in church when this kid comes and sits next to me. "Hi," he said, confident and sure of himself.

"I heard your name is Brett. My name is Brett too."

And so started the friendship of a lifetime. The other is a guy by the name of Brian, but we called him Cheez. Yes, Cheez with a "z" and no "e". I don't think it started out being spelled with a "z" but Cheez wanted to get personalized plates for his Murray dirt bike and "Cheese" would not fit. So "z" it was, thinking ahead of our time, speaking the rap dialect of future generations. Brett was a year older than me and lived in the nearby town of Dupo. Dupo just happened to

EVERYTHING ELSE

be our school's archrival so I considered Brett to be from the "wrong side of the tracks" as it was.

Because Brett was a year older than myself, he got his driver's license a year before me and suddenly, the world changed. Brett and I were interested in approximately one thing at this point: girls. Brett was bold, not scared to say anything, and he had a way with the girls. And his mullet was absolutely breathtaking. During the late 80's, the mullet was the man mane of choice. Short in the front, long in the back, the mullet is living proof that we all make mistakes. Boys made mistakes by getting them; girls made mistakes by liking them. I had a mullet for a while, spiked on top and long in the back, but like most with a mullet my hair was straight and a bit stringy. Brett, on the other hand, had the Holy Grail of mullets. He had thick hair, so instead of his hair lying on the back of his neck, he had curls and the girls loved it. He brushed his hair often and it was an amazing mane that was only rivaled by Samson of the Bible, Fabio or (deep breath, let it out, Billy Ray Cyrus).

Our summers were spent wherever girls might be found, (the pool, Six Flags or in the church youth group) and we liked our summers with Cheez, so to speak (You remember Brian?). Brian was a phenomenon. He could invent anything; the kid could take anything apart and when he put it back together it was bigger, better, and stronger, I think that Brian may have had a hand in the inventing of The Six Million Dollar Man. Brian always had big ideas, and he was an action man; act now think later. The thoughts of consequences, well, I am not even sure they made it into the single digits on his list. When we were younger, Brian figured out how to get into the cable box and hack into premium channels which was great while in high school, but was even better when we went to college together. It seemed as though whatever Brian could dream up, he could build. And he believed the word "no" was just a subtle suggestion. So with

EVERYTHING ELSE

Brett's hair, Brian's brains and whatever I could bring to the game, we were unstoppable. It is a wonder that we are still alive.

The three of us were never where we were supposed to be. It didn't matter what the situation might be. If it was a good idea for us to show up, we were definitely going to pull a no-show. If it was going to end badly, we were there early. We all went to the same church and church wasn't bad as long as it wasn't Sunday mornings. Youth group was great, mainly because there were girls there so we were all over that. But Sunday mornings we had to go to Sunday school and then to big church. Big church was long and while I am sure that our Pastor had some amazing things to say I didn't listen. At all. Before Brett had his driver's license we would wait until after the first song, then one by one, sneak out and meet in the woods behind the church. I don't even remember what we did out there, but we were definitely not in church. Then about 10 minutes before service ended we would sneak back in church, bow our heads with the closing prayer and leave with our families. It was perfect. But after Brett got his license, everything changed. We were no longer confined to the woods. We would sneak out, but it was kind of like brain surgery, complicated and a bit frightening. So one-by-one, at predetermined intervals, we would peel out of the church being careful not to run into Ollie, the church custodian. We called him Ollie North, like the military guy, because Ollie was all business. A run-in with Ollie would for sure land you in some kind of torture chamber where they dispose of kids who cut church. In this room they threaten and beat you with a hymnal until you finally confess to your sins and give up the names of the others in your gang of "Big Sinners." If the beatings didn't break you, they would pull out the big guns, the mother of all threats, the instrument that could extract the truth out of the hardest of criminals. They would tell your parents. It was important to be at a stealth level in Ollie avoidance. Let me interject here that we did, as if

EVERYTHING ELSE

it is a big surprise, get caught by Ollie and there was no Tor-Church Chamber, there was no hymnal bludgeoning and I don't even think he told our parents. But you can never be too cautious. Once Brett got his license, we would make frequent trips to Hardee's to get a biscuit and a drink before we drove back to church to assume our position of prayer before the end of church. Brett having his license was freedom. The world was our playground and there were no parents around to tell us that what we were doing (or about to do) was a bad idea.

EVERYTHING ELSE

Cornfields, a Station Wagon, & Fireworks

Brett didn't have his own car when he turned 16, so he had to use the family car. His family had a station wagon (moment of silence for the Holy Grail). We didn't realize how uncool having a station wagon was. How do you ever get a date driving a station wagon? If some dude ever comes to pick up my daughter in a station wagon the date is over, because now, as a father, I realize that while the station wagon was the Holy Grail by little kid standards, by father standards it was the off-ramp to the Highway to Hell (the actual Highway to Hell being the van). By the way, Brian had a van. One our favorite pasttime was to drive along the back roads in between the cornfields. We would open up the back window in the wagon and I am not talking the back seat windows, I'm talking the back tailgate window, half of the back tailgate, opened all the way down.

EVERYTHING ELSE

In today's cars back windows only go down halfway for safety reasons, but not during my childhood, safety was out the window, so to speak. We would open that bad boy all the way and while Brett drove Brian and I would sit in the back cargo area, light bottle rockets and shoot them out the back window. We weren't really shooting at anything, I think it just made us feel a little like Mad Max, like we had guns attached to our vehicle. This is the type of things of which boys dream. The same boys that will someday come and knock on my door asking to take my daughter away for a couple of hours in a vehicle for a night on the town. Anyway, we would shoot these bottle rockets at the occasional house as we passed by. I am not sure what we were going to go if anyone ever started chasing us down, but I am sure it would have made for a great story.

One night we ran out of bottle rockets before we ran out of night. That was when Brian, the great mind, the one we called Cheez, came up with the greatest pasttime ever: car sledding. In the station wagon you could fold the backseat forward, creating a huge cargo area that went all the way from the tailgate to just behind the driver's seat. The cargo area was a smooth painted metal of some kind. Brian took one of the floor mats and turned it over to the carpet side and he sat on it in the cargo area. Brian sitting on the opposite rubber side of the floor mat, the carpet side against the metal made it very easy to slide around the cargo area much like an air hockey mallet slides on an air hockey table. Brian would put the mat down and start all the way against the back cargo door and Brett would drive, then we would count down three, two, one and Brett would slam on the brakes.

I didn't really pay attention much in school, but one thing that I caught onto was that an object in motion tends to stay in motion. So when Brett would slam on the brakes whoever was on the carpet mat sled would come flying toward the front seats and slam into the back of them. This made for hours of fun. It was a new game so we were anything but professional Carpet Mat Sliders. Figuring out what was the perfect speed to get ramped up to before hitting the brakes was trial and error at this point.

Out of the three of us, the Brett's and a Brian, there was a nine out of ten chance, at any given time, that if somebody was going to get hurt or sustain injury from our antics it was going to be Brian. Brian was sitting in the back, assuming the ready position, and was waiting for the countdown. We were on a back road that Brett was not used to, but it was near my house, so I knew the road. We were cruising along a good clip, way above the tested measurements for maximum car sledding experimentation and development. Cornfields on both sides enclosed us. As we approached a very sharp corner that Brett was unaware of, but I of course knew it was coming.

"There's a sharp curve coming up," I said to Brett.

Maybe the music was too loud, maybe he was so focused on preparing to count down, but whatever the reason, Brett did not hear me.

"Hey, sharp corner coming up, Brett," I repeated, feeling the panic flutter in my stomach.

"Brett!" I was yelling now and by the time Brett noticed the corner we both knew there was no way he was getting that boat of a vehicle to take that corner. We were going too fast and if you know anything about station wagons, then you know they take corners like a boat, they kind of float out, not really gripping the road. You feel like the front half makes the turn and eventually the back half of the car follows. We were flying towards this corner and Brett and I both knew we were not going to make it. We knew that we were, in fact, going to be in the cornfield. Brian however, in the back of the wagon ready to sled, was blissfully unaware that there was an excellent possibility that he was about to experience a life-altering event. Brett had no choice but to slam on the brakes, but we continued hurtling toward the cornfield. I learned a second law of motion that night: that a body in motion tends to stay in motion unless acted on by an outside force. I am sure that I have seen this law at work before, but on that night, in that station wagon bouncing through that Illinois cornfield, I saw an example I will never forget.

I have no idea how fast we were going when Brett slammed on the breaks, but I know that whatever speed we were going, Brian's body on the carpet sled continued at that same speed. Brian was flying through the station wagon and the station wagon was flying through the cornfield. Brian was moving at breakneck speed on his magic carpet and ideally should have slammed into the back of the passenger seat but the cornfield ride had thrown him off course. He came flying ("an object in motion"), in between the passenger and driver's seat ("tends to stay in motion") until the combination of the dashboard and his face ("until acted on by an outside force") stopped his flight. The car came to a stop and Brian was bleeding. In any type of testing or prototype there are always casualties and Brian might be the first and last casualty of car sledding.

Brett and I prioritized quickly: get the station wagon out of the cornfield and don't get caught. And oh yeah, Brian is bleeding. We pulled into my driveway and got Brian inside and cleaned up. We processed what had happened, checked ourselves over one last time and went back out to the car to leave and the car wouldn't start. Turn the key. Nothing. Smile and turn the key. Nothing. I don't know anything about cars and neither did Brett. Brian was the only one that had some knowledge of how vehicles work, but he was in no condition for mechanic work that night. My dad was home and he was the best mechanic I have ever met. I went back inside to get my dad and told him that the car wouldn't start. He walked outside with us and Brett popped the hood. Brian was sitting in the back seat having

EVERYTHING ELSE

completely removed himself from the situation and probably thanking God he was still alive. My dad was at the front of the car and Brett and I were on either side as my dad reached and unlatched the hood Brett and I just stood there looking at the engine wondering what kind of lie we could make up to get out of this. If this had been a murder scene there was blood all over the place. When my dad opened up the hood corn stalks were everywhere. My dad looked at it and stepped back. He didn't look at us or say a word. Then he stepped forward and starting pulling corn out the engine. After several minutes of awkward silence and watching my dad pull corn out of a station wagon, he told us to give it another try. It turned over right away. My dad closed the hood and walked back into the house. He never said a word; He never made eye contact, showed no emotion, gave no sign that I was going to be in trouble later. He just walked away.

That is the kind of dad my dad is. He knows. Even when you think he doesn't know he knows and he is ok with it. He knows. And that is why God gave him sons. Boys do dumb things. We hurt each other and we hurt ourselves. For a boy growing up is one big experiment of trying to figure out how to have the most fun without dying. We are boys; the reason God made scabs, the reason why He created the human body with the ability to heal itself. We are boys; we turn things into guns. We shoot each other with these make-believe guns and sometimes we shoot each other with BB guns. We are boys; you don't have to tell us about death because we figured that out after we accidentally killed our first frog, or hacked a snake to death out of fearful surprise. We are boys and if we are blessed enough, we have dads that look the other way sometimes. We have dads that keep some secrets about what we do from our moms because if mom knew dad might get a spanking too.

Now that I am a dad, I know Graham is going to get hurt, he is going to push the envelope and we will probably have to pay a

EVERYTHING ELSE

hospital bill at some point because he did something dumb. Moms have a tough job; I would never be able to be a mom and balance all that they do. For dads, our job is trying to find the balance between what is going to get our sons injured or just hurt. It is trying to figure out the delicate balance between what Mom needs to know and what might eventually result in a constant nervous tick. For dads, it's trying to find the balance of when to teach, when to put the brakes on and when to just pull the cornstalks out of the engine and just walk away with the knowledge that we are boys; life is an adventure.

EVERYTHING ELSE

A Jeep, a Lost Boy & the Neighbors

  The neighborhood I grew up in was a tight-knit community. We were the type of neighbors that looked out for one another. We knew where everyone hid the extra key to the house in case there was an emergency. We had an older couple that lived in our neighborhood that had cowboy gear in their basement. They had metal guns with holsters, chaps and badges. They also had a collection of harmonicas. Their children were grown and gone, but they kept these toys. If we couldn't find anything to do outside, which seldom happened, we'd wander over to Joy and Gene Gray's house, the grandparents of our neighborhood. We would ring the doorbell and ask if we could play in their basement. They always said yes. What was theirs was ours. That was our neighborhood. We even shared water. We had cisterns that held rainwater. The rainwater would go through a filtering system in the basement and we would have good, clean, chemical-free water. At times when there was little or no rainfall, we had to haul water to fill

EVERYTHING ELSE

up our cisterns so we all shared a water-hauling truck. It sat in the cul-de-sac with the key underneath the floor mat. If you needed to haul water, you just took the neighborhood truck. We shared the insurance bill and you filled up the truck if it needed gas. We took care of one another. It's a way of life that slowly disappeared, it seems.

One late afternoon Brian and I noticed one of the neighborhood mothers out at the edge of the cornfield. Her mannerisms and motions told us she was upset. By the time we walked over to see what was going on, Gene and Joy and some other neighbors were already there. The mother was part of a family that was new to the neighborhood; we didn't even know their names yet. They had two children and their four year old son had walked out the back door and wandered into the cornfield. Growing up with cornfields and spending countless hours running through them there are a couple of things you have to know to be a Professional Cornfield Player.

- When the corn is still green and the leaves are fresh they have sharp edges. When running through the cornfields you would get little scrapes and cuts that you didn't even know you had until you began to sweat and the sweat would get into the little cuts and would begin to burn. This was unavoidable; it was one of the byproducts of being a Pro. To protect your face, when running, you ran with your arms in front of you.

- You can easily get lost in cornfields. As you run through a cornfield it is very important you always remember which direction that you are going. If you get turned around, the only thing you could do is scream and hope someone finds you, or you could follow a row. Let me explain. If you get turned around,

EVERYTHING ELSE

pick a row and stay on that row, no matter what. It might take awhile, but you learn that all rows end somewhere, either at the farmer's house, a break in between the fields or a road. Being Professionals, we pretty much knew all of the breaks since a nice open area in the middle of a cornfield makes for a great secret hideout. We also knew the road around us.

But for this little boy, being four years old, he was inexperienced in the ways of cornrow running and he did not know about field breaks, and God forbid he ended up by a road. The mother was sure that he had been gone, at that point, for only a couple of minutes. Brian, the neighbors and myself entered the cornfield yelling, then stopping to see if we heard a cry or whimper. We continued to walk and repeat this process for nearly an hour. We all exited the cornfield around the same time none of us with the missing boy. By this time, the father had arrived home from work early because his wife had called him. While we, the neighbors, began to hatch another plan the father walked right into the cornfield. He was wasting no time on a plan; his search was on. Things started to get a little desperate as the sun was going down. Obviously looking for a lost boy in the cornfield at dark was going to be very difficult, so time was not on our side and we were losing. Brian had a big Jeep with KC lights on the top and as it started to get dark, he pulled up in the neighbor's backyard and threw on his lights, hoping that it might provide a little help, but that is exactly what it was, little help.

At this point the boy had been gone for around an hour and a half. A little boy could go a long way in that time, especially if he was scared and running. We had also not seen anything of the boy's father since he walked into the field thirty minutes earlier. We were all at a place where we were just as lost as they were; we had no idea where to go or what to do next. We had flashlights and plenty of people, but we are talking a thousand acres of corn. As we all stood at the edge of the cornfield, Joy trying to comfort the crying mother, we heard someone coming our way through the corn. We assumed it was the father having made his way back after realizing how desperate the situation was. We stood there, watching, looking at the solid wall of corn, making it impossible to see anything beyond it as the sun went down. It was the father and when he stepped out, he was holding his son. I don't think I've ever seen a man clutching a child so tightly and with so much relief and determination.

One time, at an amusement park when Graham was around five years old, we lost Graham. We were with a group of people and each of us thought the other was keeping an eye on him. As soon as we realized Graham was not with us, I hit panic. Even while I am writing this it makes my heart hurt almost; I can still feel the fear that ran through me and Amy as we began to run through the amusement park screaming his name. There were thousands of people and it was so loud who would hear us? You don't have any idea what to do in that situation to be productive, so you do what feels right at the time: anything and everything possible to find what is missing. And what was missing was my son.

We found him at a nearby shop crying. He apparently had found a toy gun that he wanted to see and did not notice that we had walked off. Graham was missing for about five minutes, but it was one of the longest five minutes of my life. I cannot imagine parents who have had a child that has gone missing; I've only had a tiny taste of the hurt, the unanswered questions, the self-questioning and when you think about it for any good amount of time, you begin to realize why parents never give up looking. That day in the cornfield this dad stepped out with his son who had been missing for more than an hour. The mom runs to them crying and hugging them and everyone

EVERYTHING ELSE

watching can practically taste the relief. That's a beautiful image: a son that was lost, but is now found.

There are not enough fingers and toes in this town to count the number of times that I have walked away from Jesus. The number of times I have just done my own thing and every time, every single time, He finds me. The dad in this story said that he found his son sitting and crying in between the rows. The boy did nothing to help his father find him; he just sat and gave up. So many times I have felt the same way. I just sat down, quit running, totally exhausted and before I knew it Jesus had me, and carried me back, until He stepped across the blackness and into the waning light of home.

But I suppose what I truly struggle with is grace. The Father comes and finds me every time and then I feel guilty, like I owe Jesus something. Grace means owing nothing for the favor of a God that could never be repaid in the first place. He loves us simply because He loves us. I often feel the need to repay Him, to behave better, to be a good boy and every time I do this I find myself back in the cornfield. When that dad stepped out of the cornfield with his rescued child, there was only love, happiness and joy. His dad was not angry with him nor did he sit him down and give him a lecture on the dangers of Cornfield Running. Only joy. So why do I feel like Jesus is mad at me? Because as humans, we operate on a spectrum of emotions while Jesus operates on love. And He feels that love every time He brings me out of the cornfield. It's the same joy that I felt once I saw Graham in that store standing next to the clerk. It overcame me. All that mattered was finding him and getting him back to where he belonged, with Amy and me. Next time you wander into the cornfield, and there will be a next time, know that grace has you. You will be found; Jesus loves you and holds you this time and the next and the next and the next.

EVERYTHING ELSE

Zippers, Dancing & Graduation

My eighth grade year was maybe my finest, or at least in my head it was my finest. Currently I am 5'10.5" and the half makes all the difference, I promise. When I was in eighth grade I was 5'10, so in the last 20 years I have grown a half of an inch. I wish I was taller but when I was in eighth grade, 5'10" was taller than most other kids in my grade and I thought this was amazing. Junior high is filled with awkwardness: you're growing, you're feet are getting bigger, you're kind of clumsy, you're body is changing in other ways that make locker rooms awkward or standing up in front of a group even more awkward at times. As if these moments aren't bad enough for some guys, junior high is when you get that first real girlfriend.

Some of us might have had those elementary school flings with the girl who sat next to us in Miss Mayberry's class who might have been named DeeDee. I am, of course, talking about myself. We started "going steady" in fifth grade. It started like any typical romantic relationship. Our relationship would probably make for a

EVERYTHING ELSE

great Nicholas Sparks novel. It went something like this. We had the school parade and fair coming up and I wanted a girl to go with, because Ferris wheels are better ridden with a partner, and if you want that ride to be even better, your partner should be a female. So there I am, looking for a girl, when my friend Jason informs me that he has two girlfriends and that he can't very well take them both to the fair. So out of the kindness of his heart he let me borrow one of his girlfriends and I got DeeDee in the deal.

That sounds so awful now that I think back on it, but I promise at the time it was totally innocent. So started a beautiful relationship... DeeDee and I went to that fair and rode the Ferris wheel and it was beautiful. I can't remember if I mentioned yet that I have a fear of heights so the only thing I can remember about that ride is the fact that I wanted it to be over; besides DeeDee was more beautiful with two feet on the ground.

But DeeDee was just a loaner, and we both knew that it wouldn't last. So fast-forward to the real first relationship: eighth grade was great for me, as I mentioned. I felt as if I was getting a little more attention that I used to. I was not the most popular in my class, nor was I the least. Out of 100 kids, I would say that my class ranking in popularity stats would have been around 25, top quarter, not bad. But there was this period in eighth grade when my stock skyrocketed, definitely encroaching on the top ten until my ranking took a bit of a hit after a party out at DeeDee's house. We had moved on from each other; we were so over the Ferris wheel. DeeDee had a bon-fire out at her house and it was here that I would drop a couple of points in the popularity poll. I had a new girl, Jennifer, eighth grade, cheerleader, blonde...you know, the type of girl that only top-10ers can get. We hung around the bonfire for a bit, but at some point we had moved to sit on a hillside together.

EVERYTHING ELSE

It was the deep stuff that we were taking into consideration as we sat on that hillside talking about where we might end up in this world. But while we were counting stars and counting our blessings I was counting down in my head from ten to zero and at zero I would make my move; THE move. I was going to give Jennifer a kiss, a kiss that she would never forget. I was absolutely positive that when we kissed a star would streak across the sky and the bonfire would explode in a fiery ball of passion, igniting us in flame and smoke for the entire eighth grade to witness. And Jennifer would be mine forever.

It was time; we were ready. We had been heavily involved for two or three days. If ever a couple was ready to take it to the next level, it was us. I had counted down from ten to zero eight or nine times trying to get up the nerve, time it perfect, waiting for her to say a word that started with "W" because that is the perfect kissing letter. Like "where" or "watermelon." (You did it didn't you? You said "where" or "watermelon", it works every single time. Sucker...)

I finally made my move; I kissed her and it was magic. My heart thumped and it left me breathless. I moved away slowly to let the moment linger in the air for just a bit. I just knew when I opened my eyes Jennifer's eyes would still be closed because she didn't want the moment to end and she would be replaying the scene over and over again in her pretty little head. But when I opened my eyes, a lazy smile playing on my lips, her eyes were not shut, they were wide open and she was looking at me. What she said next I can never forget:

"I am going to go back to the bonfire."

There are no "W" words in that phrase. She wanted to go back? She wanted to leave this magical paradise that my lips had created for us? How did this happen? The rest of the evening was filled me following her around as she tried to ignore me. That was on a Saturday night. On Monday I missed school because I was sick, and when I returned to school on Tuesday I found out that Jennifer had broken up with me and I didn't even know it until after lunch.

I went through the first half of the day thinking I had a girlfriend while in actuality she had broken up with me and I didn't even know it because she didn't tell me. So goes junior high relationships: you can be dating and not know it, be broken up and not know it and your magical moment can be someone else's nightmare. I feel the need now to apologize to Jennifer; I am sure whatever she experienced that night at DeeDee's is burned in her mind for a totally different reason.

Don't worry, I came back from that experience stronger, although I never could get another eighth grade girl to date me again so I decided to do what no other eighth grader before me had done. I asked a girl to go steady with me, to be my girlfriend. I retaliated against the entire eighth grade by going steady with a seventh grader and the eighth grade girls were livid. (This girl also broke up with me, although she at least decided to let me actually know that we were no longer dating.)

After this girl I turned my attention to a girl that was one of my best friends. On the phone one night I told her my true feelings; I told her that she was a great friend and that I couldn't fight that feeling any longer. Yes, in my quest to be suave, I sang a song made popular by REO Speedwagon. The response that I received from her was a phrase that I would get used to over the years:

"Brett you are such a nice guy. I don't want to ruin what we have. I just want to be friends." Translation: not a chance. Now I know up to this point this year sounds bad, but listen, the fact that I was even in the position to ask a girl out was a pretty amazing place to be. Eighth grade all points to the end of the year graduation dance.

EVERYTHING ELSE

This was our last hurrah, all of our misdeeds, all of the "I just want to be friends" brush-offs, all of them could be made mere memories because legends were born during the eighth grade graduation dance. I believe I took a girl (although I am not sure) but what I do know is that Cheez and I walked in together. We came into junior high together and we were going out together.

The dance was held in our school gymnasium and when you entered our gym, you would come through the double doors that were up three steps of stairs. So when you entered you were elevated above the gym floor like a small porch before you would take the steps down onto the gym floor. This was the exact set of stairs and gym that I would enter every day because it was also where we had lunch. While you were eating lunch the doors would fly open and all eyes would swing to the stage to see who was coming in. These were the same stairs that, when I was in fifth grade I had a broken foot, which meant I had a cast. Everyone knows that a cast means attention because girls like to sign casts. I had crutches and I was cool. Because I was on crutches, Mrs. Day let me be the line leader going to lunch. All the cool kids wanted to be line leaders and since I was the line leader, any doubt that I was, in fact, very cool was erased.

The first day on crutches was amazing; lots of questions, lots of signatures, then it was lunchtime. I led that class like a champ; the click of the crutches followed by my foot hitting the tile floor was like a champion's anthem announcing my arrival. As we approached the gym the double doors were shut. Mrs. Day flung open one door while the lunch helper threw open the other door and all eyes turned to the stairs to see who was entering. All of those third and fourth graders looked at me, the line leader with crutches and a cast and with obvious swagger. I moved inside the door to the small porch and steps. The house I grew up in was a ranch with an unfinished

EVERYTHING ELSE

basement so I had no reason to go down there so up until this point in my crutches experience I had no working knowledge

of how you should go down steps.

Crutches first or feet first? The pressure was on. Everyone was watching and I had to make a choice; I had a 50/50 shot of getting this right. That day, I chose poorly. I went feet first. When making the wrong choice on crutches you realize fairly quickly that you indeed made the wrong choice. I was now dangling from my armpits on the crutches as they slowly began to tip toward the gym floor, three steps down. It was a slow fall until I ended up face first on the gym floor.

So these are the same doors and entryway that Cheez and I were about to walk through for the last time, one last chance to set this place on fire. I had a double breasted, gray plaid, short coat suit, turquoise tie (skinny), blue shirt, and fake patent leather shoes that I am pretty sure had fake alligator skin on the side with a silver tip toe. I was a cross between a Tommy Hilfiger ad and the Fresh Prince of Bel-Air. The hair parted down the middle and way too much Drakkar were the final touches on my last junior high ensemble and this was our moment. The doors opened up and we take a step forward. I put my hands in my pockets and so did Cheez. We were like Sonny and Crockett from Miami Vice just surveying the scene, looking for the victims… if you know what I mean.

I checked myself and I was looking goooooood. Then I looked over to double check Cheez. His zipper was all the way down. I mean ALL the way and with his hands in his pockets there might as well have been a neon sign slowly and brightly blinking "open, open, o-p-e-n." Let's talk in terms of leaving the barn door open: his barn was all door and off its hinges. His zipper was open so far that you can see his tucked in shirt through the open zipper. I didn't want to make a scene, so I looked away still nodding, much like the Night at the

EVERYTHING ELSE

Roxbury guys. Over the music, without even making eye contact, I told Brian. It had to be done this way. You had to play this cool. So with head nodding I just said, "Cheez, your zipper is down," but he did not play it so cool. He immediately spun around and closed the barn door. That was the last time I ever walked through those doors. I think God makes us go through junior high to pay for past and future sins.

EVERYTHING ELSE

EVERYTHING ELSE

Homecoming, a Jerk & a Girl

During one of my homecomings when I was in high school, I stood a girl up. Maybe I was using her to get back at all the times girls told me they just wanted to be friends. I promise when I tell you what I did, you may shut this book right where you are, burn it and send me nasty hate mail. There was a girl I had met at church camp one year. (Church camp was always one of the finest places to pick up a summer romance.) When I say "I met" her I mean that actually "Brett met" her then I talked to her on the phone because Brett had too many other girls to keep track of so he let me borrow Melinda. It was DeeDee, the sequel.

     She was from another youth group and lived about 30 miles from us, so we just talked on the phone. I finally got the nerve one time to ask her out on a date and to my surprise, she said yes. I didn't really know what to do with a "yes" but we went on a date. I took my parents' white Chevy Celebrity with maroon cloth interior and a bench seat in the front. I don't even know if they make bench seats in

EVERYTHING ELSE

cars anymore, but in my day, bench seats were made for girls to slide over and sit right next to you while you were driving, that is if everything was going well. I went on one other date once and as soon as we got in the car the girl slid over next to me right from the get go! I was so excited I almost threw up! But there wasn't any room because she was sitting right next to me! We never went on another date…

But here I was with my parents' Celebrity making the 30 mile drive to her house. Let me remind you that I only met this girl once at church camp; all other communication was done over the phone. There was no Facebook to look up pictures or texting to send pics. There was the only hope that maybe one of the many pictures you took at camp had her in it or that you could get hold of the yearbook from the school she attended. I found her house, walked up the sidewalk and rang the doorbell. There was that awkward moment of silence while you wait to hear footsteps coming to the door. She answered the door. "Hi," I said, nervous enough that the arches of my feet were sweating. "Oh!" I could read the surprise in her voice, but I didn't know if it was good or bad. I soon found out. "I thought you were going to be the other Brett", she said. How do you come back from that? I was the wrong Brett, I had already failed her before I started. Somehow, I salvaged the date and even ended up asking her to my Homecoming.

You might, because you have grown to identify with me and have probably become more than a little attached to me, be asking what I possibly did wrong. You may be thinking that in this little love story Melinda is the villain. Just wait. It's coming… Melinda and I continued to talk on the phone, but in the weeks leading up to Homecoming what little flame we might have had was dying; I am not even sure if the match was smoking anymore.

EVERYTHING ELSE

Melinda played tennis and the day of Homecoming she had a tennis tournament so she was going to be pushing it to make it in time. The plan was, she was going to call me when she got home from her match so that I could be making the 30 mile drive while she got ready. We had dinner reservations for 6 pm so we could make it to the dance by 7:30 pm. As the day wore on, I found myself dreading the night that was slowly gaining on me and regretting that I had ever made plans to go to Homecoming with a girl at all. I had some friends that were going stag and I really wanted to go hang out with them. Time went by, 5:30 pm and no phone call. In my head I was thinking she wasn't even home from the tennis match yet, I have a 30 mile drive there and a 30-mile drive back and there is no way we would make it to dinner. Then it occurred to me that maybe Melinda wasn't even home and didn't want to go.

During the day, I had started talking on the phone with another girl who had no date and who was a good friend. Let's just say it might be possible, maybe there was a chance that possibly without knowing what I was doing, during the course of the conversation with this other girl, my friend, I may have asked her to go with me to Homecoming as well. Maybe. So I was double booked, you see. In my head it made perfect sense; this girl was going to be too late to go, I would go with my friend, get to the dance and hang out with my guy friends and then we were going to go camping. It was perfect.

Around 5:35 pm. Melinda called and that was okay. I figured she was calling to say she was sorry she was so late and that I should go alone because it will be too late for me to drive there and pick her up. That didn't happen. What she did say was this: "Hey Brett! I'm ready!" and she sounded excited.

I sat there speechless for a second, then I told her that I didn't think I was going to go. Apparently she was speechless as well

EVERYTHING ELSE

because there was only silence. Then there wasn't: "What do you mean? I got ready, I bought a dress for your homecoming and everything." She was upset. She was really, really upset. Not knowing what to say I simply told her I had to go and then I hung up. Right before I hung up on her I heard her dad tell her to give him the phone so that he could talk to me.

Now that I have a daughter, I realize that if I had indeed talked to him on the phone he would have reached through the phone and punched me and I wouldn't blame him. I am not proud of that moment, but it happened; I feel a little better confessing it finally.

I went to Homecoming with my friend, had dinner, hung out with my friends at the dance and then we went camping. The story doesn't end here though, because that would be simple and easy and I would have gotten away with it... smooth criminal.

While at the dance I started talking to another girl, who happened to live right down the road from where we were going to go camping. We brewed a plan that at around midnight, I would walk down to her house and shine a light in her window, then she would sneak out and we would just hang out for a while. It was all very innocent... probably. Midnight arrived and Cheez, our friend Shaun and I made our way down the road and up her driveway. We were hiding behind some bushes and I got my flashlight, shined it into her window and waited for her to come to the window. Then something funny happened. It wasn't funny at the time, but now it is. The curtains ruffled and someone appeared, but it wasn't my pretty little lady love. It was her father. We scrambled, sprinting down the road. Cheez was never the athletic one, but that night, powered by the fear of what that man was going to do to us, Cheez was flying down the road leading me. It wasn't until we got back to the campsite that we realized

EVERYTHING ELSE

Shaun was not with us anymore. Cheez and I made it almost all the way back to our campsite, (which was in Shaun's backyard) and then we saw Shaun's dad come out of their house, get in his car and take off down their driveway. There was no doubt that Shaun had been caught. We sprinted the rest of the way up through his yard into the backyard and into the tent. Several minutes later Shaun's dad came driving back up the driveway with Shaun in the passenger seat. It is one thing to be in trouble from your own parents; it is totally another thing to get in trouble from someone else's parents. Shaun's dad got out of the car told me and Cheez to follow him in the house. His parents didn't yell or scream and I don't remember specifically what they even said to us, except for one thing. At the end of the late night early morning conference Shaun's mother looked at me and Cheez and said that we had until noon the next day to tell our parents the truth. She said that at noon she would call our parents to make sure they knew the whole story. I would rather be spanked by someone else's parents than have to tell my parents what had just happened.

The next day was church. We always went to church, even after standing up a perfectly nice girl on Homecoming night, camping out with friends, getting caught by a girl's father and being blackmailed by a soccer mom we went to church. Cheez's mom and my mom were sitting together. They asked if we had fun, we smiled and said approximately the following: oh yeah, we did, we had a great dinner out and the dancing, then we tried sneaking over to a girl's house and her father found us and Cheez and I beat feet back to Shaun's but left Shaun there like the sacrificial lamb but it was no big deal because we are young and wild spirited boys whom you love. We did the verbal equivalent of a kid trying to hide his green beans under his mashed potatoes. Both of our mothers said, "stop" and we were caught again. I am pretty sure we smooth talked our moms into

EVERYTHING ELSE

thinking it was no big deal and just a big misunderstanding (and Shaun's mother totally bluffed us, she never even called our parents.) But now I have my own daughter and there are these boys around. Boys that someday will want to meet with her late at night without me knowing. I try to tell Tyler every chance I get that boys are bad and they smell funny. They do gross things like picking their noses and eat their boogers and these are the same boys with the same lips that are going to want to kiss her someday with their booger lips. Boys do dumb things like seeing who can pee the longest distance when they are out in the woods. Boys think about gross things. Boys have diseases that will never go away until they are 40, some even longer. Tyler currently is pretty infatuated with Justin Beiber and I am okay with that; he is a long way away and the chances of Justin Bieber coming up my driveway are slim.

    Right now Tyler is in love with her daddy. I tell Tyler how beautiful she is all the time and how I am in love with her heart. We go on Daddy-Daughter dates and I open doors and pull out chairs and never get out my phone, unless I am taking a picture of the two of us together. I am going to make it very difficult for some boy to out do me someday. I know there will be some boy some day that will come and steal her heart, but until that day comes I am making sure that no one tells her she is beautiful more than me. I figure I have a head start on all the boys her age that are in this world.

    Amy does an amazing job teaching and showing her what a real lady looks and acts like and she has not avoided difficult discussions with her. One time on the way back from a trip to Charlotte, Tyler asked Amy about sex. Amy told her as much as a 10 year old needed to know, enough that she began to understand what sex was. Tyler loves babies and one day while we were grabbing a bite to eat at Firehouse Subs there was a mom that walked in with a newborn. Amy was looking at the baby and Tyler was talking about

EVERYTHING ELSE

how beautiful the baby was then Amy jokingly said she wanted to have another baby. Had this been Tyler during the pre-sex talk years, she would have been all for it, but this time when Amy said it, Tyler took a step back, looked at us both and then said in a voice loud enough for the other people in line to hear, "Well, now that I know how that process works, no thank you!" Most days, as a dad, I have no idea what I am doing. I am just making it up as I go and hoping my kids don't end up too jacked up. I know that just like some day some boy will come and steal my little girl's heart, there also will be boys that will break her heart. There will be boys that will ditch her when she has taken so much time to find the right dress and put every hair in the right place, but when those boys do come I will be there and she will always know that her dad believes that she is the most beautiful thing ever, just like her momma.

EVERYTHING ELSE

EVERYTHING ELSE

Hearing Aids, Aliens and Tumors

When I was young my father was healthy; he worked, he played catch and he wrestled with my brother and me. I don't remember anything ever being wrong with him, except for the time he passed out in the bathroom and received the great slapping from my mother. The next time that he passed out I was in junior high and I was spending the night at Brett's house. We got up on Sunday morning to go to church because our family always went to church, no matter what. That morning, Brett's mother told me that my mom had called and wanted to let me know they would not be coming to church that morning because my dad "wasn't feeling well." I knew something was wrong; my parents never missed church. Jesus was taking attendance and keeping a tight record on who missed, how many times you missed and why you missed. While being sick was a valid excuse, unlike boating, or sleeping in, I knew something else was wrong.

EVERYTHING ELSE

When I got home that morning my mom told me the story: earlier they were getting ready to go to church when my father passed out again, fell against the fridge and landed in the dog's water bowl. I suppose it should have been funny, but something in my gut told me this time, there wouldn't be laughing. They went to the doctor and ran some tests, did some scans and that is when our family found out that my dad had a rare disease called Neurofibromatosis Type 2.

The disease is marked by non-cancerous brain tumors that, in the majority of cases, grow out of the auditory nerve. The tumors can cause facial paralysis, balance issues and most of the time leave the victim profoundly deaf. My dad has been hard of hearing for as long as I could remember, but as far as I knew, all dads were hard of hearing, just like all dads that were dealing with male-pattern baldness wore toupees. There were very specific guidelines for being a father in the 1980's and my father was one of the authors of the handbook. Of course, my father only wore his toupee on Sunday because it's a little known fact that Jesus had an aversion to bald men in the house of the Lord. Remember the Sabbath and keep it holy, but cover up your bald spots because there's a difference between "holy" and "holey." In all honesty, the toupee fascinated me in the same way one is fascinated by a snake ball. I once asked a friend if he wanted to see my dad's rug and I took him into the bathroom opened the drawer and there it lay, looking like a fresh piece of road kill or a bear rug for doll houses. My dad found out I showed it to my friend with the kind of fascinated horror that a kid with a quarter to spend would approach a sideshow freak behind a curtain and he stopped wearing it.

Being hard of hearing was the true mark of a Laxton: my mother and my uncle both were almost completely deaf. My dad, my grandmother and my other uncle all wore hearing aids before hearing aids were science fiction-esque sophisticated pieces of life-assisting technology. In fact, sitting amongst them was like playing Russian

EVERYTHING ELSE

roulette with your sanity due to the high-pitched squelch of feedback that could come from one or all of them at any given time... or at the same time. When all three of them would converge upon our dinner table it was like the hearing aids were talking with one another in some high-pitched alien babble. One would squeal and we would bump Dad and tap our ear, the terrestrial signal that we were being slowly brain-stabbed by his squealing hearing aid. He would adjust, we would regain control over our nervous systems and then Grandma's would start in, and before you could bump her and give her the sign my uncle's would start only to be answered by my dad's again, like a choir of ear bleeding high-pitched choruses. After a while we would just give up and give in to the horror. I am not sure why they even wore them; I don't remember them helping all that much. We couldn't get the deaf ones to listen to us because they were too busy talking loud enough so they could hear each other. Asking for the salt or the gravy resulted simply in having everything near them passed to you until you finally got what you wanted. Looking back, I don't know why we didn't make cue cards so they knew what item to pass. I wonder what it must have looked like to outsiders who often visited with our family.

I pray for them to this day. During my freshman year in high school, my dad had his first brain surgery. It left him with one side of his face paralyzed, his balance messed up and deaf on one side. The only hearing he had left was out of one ear and he was almost completely deaf in that ear. My dad has had countless surgeries since and is now profoundly deaf and his face is almost totally paralyzed. But through everything he kept his sense of humor.

Most people who meet my father after all of his surgeries think he is a quiet man that doesn't talk much, but that is not the father I grew up with. His first surgery left him with a small percentage of hearing, but still able to communicate with his family. My parents are

EVERYTHING ELSE

people of habit, as I guess we all are to a degree, and that habitual lifestyle made communication easier. Every night we always had dinner at the same time together at the dinner table. It was always the same routine: my brother, dad and I would sit in the living room and watch TV while we waited for my mom to finish dinner.

The universal sign that dinner was almost ready was the making of the salads. When my mother was done making salads she would half-holler into the living room: "Dick come get the ice out."

Getting the ice out meant that Dad was going to fix the drinks and it was time to come to the table. You could have set your clocks by this daily routine. Until the day you couldn't. Like most things in life, chance or choice leads the order of the day. That day, we were in the living room, waiting for supper, my brother on the love seat to the right of my dad, Dad and I on the couch. We heard the salad bowls and knew what would come next.

"Dick come get the ice out," my mother called, still fiddling in the kitchen and as always, right on time.

My dad didn't move; Mark and I had no idea what to do. It was highly unlikely that he didn't hear her, even though he was mostly deaf. It may have been very likely he didn't know the exact words she said but as a man of routine and intelligence we figured that he could use contextual clues to determine that it was time to get the ice. He just stared at the TV. Mark and I looked at him and waited for him to move to get the ice. He didn't… still. Mom hollered out the signal once again:

"Dick, come get the ice out!"

Mark and I were fixed on dad, staring at him, expecting him to move. He didn't. He kept his eyes on the TV. There was a part of me that wanted to tap my dad and let him know it was time. But we knew that he knew and he knew that we knew that he knew. It was a Mexican standoff. It was all coming down to this moment. The only

EVERYTHING ELSE

thing in the house not sweating was the ice, because it hadn't been gotten out and put in the glasses by Dick.

"Dick, come get the ice out!" Mom was done with the salads and she was ready to eat. My dad again did not move. Then, without taking his eyes off the TV, Dad quietly let us know that some things would never change, including his sense of humor. "Its great being deaf," he mumbled just loud enough for me and my brother to hear.

This is one of my favorite memories of my father. My dad was still funny, despite all of the medical issues we had faced and were going to face in the future. Circumstance was not going to change what he was in his heart. He was the rock; he was the reason everything was going to be okay and he was not going to go away, in any way, shape or form, because of a couple of brain tumors. To my father, his wife and family were the most important things in the world and he made sure that we knew it. It was so embedded in me that once, before a surgical procedure, he got a little heated with one of the nurses because they wanted him to take off his wedding band. He never took off his wedding ring. I am 39 years old and I have never seen him without his wedding ring on. The ring, like his commitment to his wife, was and is permanent.

We were sitting on the couch one evening and there was a segment on TV about some televangelist who, as it turned out, was a total fake. Everything he had done had been a scam. He had set himself apart from his counterparts by claiming to be a healer. Trying to be funny, I told my dad we should have taken him to that man and he could have been healed. My dad is a man of few words, but when he did speak it was either going to be funny or there was a lesson in his words. Most of the time it was funny, but this night there was a lesson to be learned. He looked at me and smiled.

EVERYTHING ELSE

"It's not that I don't believe God can heal me, I know He can if He so chooses, but if this is what I have to go through to bring my family and me closer to Him, then it is worth it. This is not my home."

The disease that we found inside my father those many years ago, NF2 for short, is hereditary. My grandmother had it, my uncle had it, my dad, my brother and I all ended up with this disease. My grandmother was nearly deaf by the time she died; my father is deaf, my uncle became deaf just before he passed, my brother is hard of hearing and I have been left with 35 percent hearing in one ear only. My brother and I face a future of being profoundly deaf, but yet I know it's going to be okay. I know that being hard of hearing is tough, but it can be funny, just like my dad.

This past year I bought my first hearing aid. Let me tell you this: if being a parent doesn't suck all of the cool right out of your life, try wearing a hearing aid. Nothing screams "YOU ARE OLDER THAN DIRT!" like wearing one of these bad boys. Modern advancements have done away with all of the squealing and alien talk, but there is no way to walk into a store and buy hearing aid batteries and come off as the cool dad, the hipster dude, the distinguished 30-something that everyone strives to be as they slowly age past what they were into what they are going to be, no matter what. Sometimes when I buy the batteries I pick up a Monster energy drink and try to casually drop that I'm buying the batteries for my dad hoping that the teenage clerk with all of that still intact hearing will believe me and not think that I am totally irrelevant to the world that they live in.

I had my first brain surgery four years ago. I can't really play basketball anymore; I walk like I am drunk most days and in most conversations I understand enough to piece together sentences and hope that I am talking about the same subject as everyone else, but it's okay. No, I'm not saying that to be the "bigger man," or the martyr. It really is okay. Through all of this I have a deeper understanding of

EVERYTHING ELSE

God's faithfulness. I have a deeper understanding of how beautiful the church can be as I saw her people rally around my family when my dad was going through his surgeries and I saw them rally around my wife and kids during mine. I have a deeper affection for those that are my friends because they were there for me and my wife and kids. It's okay because this is not my home and I have the faith that one day there will be no more surgeries or tumors, no more sickness. I know one day all will be made perfect and I know one day I will never have to walk into a store and buy hearing aid batteries, or Monster energy drinks. But just so you know, all the cool people are wearing hearing aids these days.

EVERYTHING ELSE

College Years

College was one of the most amazing times of my life. It was where I found a renewed affection for Jesus, found the friends that I still call friends today and it is where I found my beautiful bride. I barely made it to college though. I was a slacker… the lifelong kind that the secret society of teachers who track slackers start a file on just after kindergarten. It's not that I wanted to be a slacker, but I just didn't see the relevance of an education centered around counting apples that you're just going to give away to some chick. I am an instant gratification guy. Why bother with something today if it isn't going to make things better today? Why do today what can wait until tomorrow? This was basically my formula for life all the way through my primary and secondary educational career. I never made the honor roll. I didn't see how that was going to help out in the future either. If you were one of those people who got to walk around on graduation day with those glorified curtain tie back ropes on your robe signifying that you were one of the smart ones then congratulations on your super long tassel thingy. I figured that all of the diplomas looked the same other than the recipient name. Really my philosophy was quite existential: I was going to merely exist and see if I could still make it. (See what I did there... THAT is the kind of intelligence you don't get in school...) This plan was amazing, groundbreaking, even, until I got ready to graduate from high school. I learned three deeply important words at that point: GPA (NOT a forerunner of GPS, not even distantly related) SAT (which I used to think was just something to do on the couch) and ACT (which was used a lot in sentences with my name and usually included an "up" or an "out" succeeding as in "Brett has a tendency to ACT up.") Turns out I was so wrong. I had made plans to go to an area college that didn't care about all that stuff, but my parents still wanted me to take the ACT. I tried to talk my parents into letting me take a year off of school before I started college but they insisted I start immediately Looking back I am glad they did because I am pretty sure one year would have turned into two, then into eight, then into being served mac and cheese in a Styrofoam bowl by your mother who tells you every day that she still believes in you, but you have to cover your ears at night as you sleep in the basement, decorated with Christmas lights and posters of boy bands because the sound of her crying echoing through the ventilation system makes you feel like a puppy kicker. From there it would definitely have been a cardboard box in greater downtown Columbia, IL.

    The Saturday I went to take my ACT, I was angry. A waste of a perfectly good Saturday morning, sitting in a classroom reading questions I didn't understand and filling in bubbles to answers that I would ultimately guess. I went through several questions, at least 10, and I didn't know a single answer. I mean I was clueless. it was maybe after question 10 that I noticed I was guessing at all of these answers. That's when it hit me. Don't get your hopes up; it wasn't that shining moment of breakthrough glory that you are waiting for. It didn't finally hit me that I had to grow up, or try harder. What hit me was more of an existentialist realization: the test existed, I existed, we existed without each other and I didn't really need to absorb the tests existence to define or reaffirm mine. That being said, why waste time reading it and then guessing when I could get the same results by just coloring in the bubbles and skipping that whole reading thing? That, my friends, is the way a true slacker thinks. I had heard it said before that if you didn't know that answer always guess "C." I am sure I read this in a great thinkers' book or possibly the Bible. Certainly Jesus would be all for this because there's a book in the Bible, one of the gospels even, called Mark. And C just happens to be the Roman numeral for 100 and if you look up the one hundredth verse of Mark it is Mark 3:29 which says, but whoever blasphemes against the Holy Spirit will never be forgiven; they are guilty of an eternal sin." To "blaspheme" means "to curse" and what letter, pray tell, does "curse" start with? You got it, a "C." Thank me later for that scriptural revelation about standardized testing…

So "C" it was. All the way up and down that little bubble sheet, I marked in the holy grail of guesses: C. In some of the sections they had more columns for answers than they did questions, but this was the DaVinci Code of test taking… they got a "C" as well. I was given three and a half hours to complete the ACT; I finished in 30 minutes. And the angels in heaven sang a sweet, sweet lullaby of victory as I put my pencil down and took a nap. I am sure the other kids were thinking this dude is a genius, but they could have been thinking this dude is a moron. It didn't matter, I was done and my parents were off my back. I scored a 15 on that bad boy, not bad for all C's.

I ended up going away to a small Baptist college, Hannibal LaGrange. It has since become a university, but back then it was just a

EVERYTHING ELSE

college. I am not sure why or how they accepted me, (it had to have been God), but they did. It was there that I met two of my closest friends: Doug and Ryan. And they couldn't have been more different. Doug had grown up in the church, but when I met him he was mad at God, bitter and angry. That is what he wore on the outside, in front of others, but when alone, he was a different person, kind and gentle, but he battled the Lord and to the outside world, and especially to the Bible majors, he was scary. He had a short temper and was always looking for a fight. One night during the annual Midnight Breakfast to celebrate finals being over, he put his arm through the window of the door and we had to hold him off of the Dean of Students.

Ryan was a preacher's kid and had grown up moving around so he didn't have very many close friends. He was reserved, quiet, and the most confident person I had ever met and I needed that. When I headed off to college, I made up my mind that I was going to reinvent myself by being myself. I was going to be the real me: outgoing and funny.

Amy

My junior year of college, (it was either my third junior year or fourth junior year), everything changed for me. I met the woman I was going to marry. Eventually she would figure that out, but the first day of school when a couple of us walked over to Kleckner Hall and started checking out the new girls it didn't take more than one moment after roaming into her room and seeing her sitting there for me to fall, heart first in love. But these things take time. She was young, just a freshman. She needed someone gentle and patient. Too bad she got me.

"So who are you?" I looked at her with what I hoped was interested disinterest.

"Amy," She replied. I knew there were an awful lot of Amy's floating around that year and I also knew her last name started with a "G." Now I knew I had to play it cool; I had to say something…

"Oh, so can I call you Amy G?"

"Sure," she responded with a tone that dripped with disinterest. The underlying tone told me that she hoped we wouldn't be around each other enough for me to call her anything. But in my head it was over.

"Oh, yes, she will be mine," I nodded my head at my friend after vacating her dorm room.

Amy had a boyfriend, and a lesser man would have given up. I was not a lesser man, not when the woman of my dreams was on the line. She was not going to be a simple conquest; the perfect ones never are.

A couple of nights later, without me knowing it, my friend that introduced mw and Amy did some recon, without my knowledge.

"So how serious are you and your boyfriend?" he asked her one night in the cafeteria. Her response was the kind of burn that you could toast marshmallows with.

"It depends on who is asking," Amy replied. "If it is that Brett guy, then we are serious."

I had been rejected without my knowledge or permission. But it's so much easier to ask forgiveness than it is to ask permission and so I hung around Amy all the time. I was like a leech and apparently it worked. We started talking and taking late night walks. Having always been void of the part of your brain that tells you to take things slow, I spilled my soul to her. I jumped in like a canonball. I have no idea why she didn't run away. She must have thought I was a nutcase. A year later I proposed, she said yes and then another year later she answered the call from God to take on the life-long mission project: Marriage to Brett Laxton. I had said earlier that Ryan was the most confident person I had ever met, but that was until I met Amy. Amy was the first girl I ever met that was cocky, (and she hates it that I say that.) But when I say that she was cocky, I mean she was cocky in the right way. She wasn't desperate. She wasn't clingy. She wasn't willing to trade off parts of her heart because she was lonely. She was certain of who she was, not just in this world but also in God. She was

EVERYTHING ELSE

and still is cocky in the best way, confident and beautiful and unbreakable, but still with a sense of compassion and softhearted love and warmth. I want my daughter to be cocky like her Mama, proud of whom God has made her to be, and confident in whom she is. I want boys to be intimidated by her; I want her to be just like her Mama.

EVERYTHING ELSE

EVERYTHING ELSE

A Drunk, Bible Majors and Beauty

The story of my friend Doug can only be called a miracle. Doug wan an angry man but really only when people were around. When alone he was hurt, sad and bitter. "Christians" on campus talked about Doug and avoided him and I can't really blame them. Most of the time when he was angry they were the targets of his anger. He needed a change and he knew it. One summer he went away to be a counselor at a church camp. How he got the invite, I will never know; but he did.

The Christmas before that summer, Doug had tanked. It was around noon and he was just getting out of bed. He was fighting a hangover from the night before and for him the best way to fight the hangover was the hair of the dog: drink more of what had gotten him there in the first place. He opened a beer and sat down on a chair next to a frazzled, pathetic Christmas tree featuring an array of dip cans and beer cans as the ornaments and a bra as the tree topper. The house was a mess from the previous night (or nights) of parting and

EVERYTHING ELSE

Doug was a mess. He was wearing a pair of gym shorts and a wife-beater that looked like it had not been washed in weeks. Doug and I had not talked in quite some time. He had gone so far off the deep end and been so angry that I had to step away for a bit. It really came to a peak one night when we all lived together in an old house. He was arguing with his twin brother in the kitchen (which was nothing new.) Amy and I were sitting in the dining room trying to study (one of the perks of loving Amy was being drawn into her study habits that were superior to mine). Their fight continued to escalate and Doug was threatening bodily hare to his kinder, gentler borther.

I couldn't take any more so I stood up and said something about their constant arguing. Doug wheeled around and looked at me with anger and sadness deep in his eyes and leaking out of every pore in his body. "F@&! You!" His eyes glowed with more than hatred; he had reached a point of indifference. I had never been on the receiving end of Doug's wrath before and my first thought was that he was going to kill me. But then, as I stood looking at what bitterness and anger had done to my friend, it was hurt that welled up and overthrew fear. I had been there for Doug and defended him when there was no defense for his actions. I had been angry with some of the Bible majors as they hated on Doug. I had sat in empty rooms with Doug while he cried and talked about his hurts.

My pain was short lived, for as soon as the words came out of his mouth I could tell that what he said hurt him too. He didn't mean it; it was just his anger spilling out. He walked to the front porth and I followed him. He had his wallet in his hand and in his anger he threw it on the ground. Pictures, identity cards, money, a whole life went flying all over the yard. He sat there on the porch and cried and apologized. Amy came outside and picked up everything from his wallet and placed them back where they belonged. I remember how I felt as she picked up all the pieces from the lawn. She was doing

EVERYTHING ELSE

what a servant would do and I hadn't seen that side of her before. She was very black and white, no shades of gray, and she didn't really have patience for people acting out in dumb ways, but her compassion that night spilled out much like the contents of Doug's wallet. In the years Amy and I have been together, I have watched her love and compassion for people grow into a full on love for Jesus and people. I would need that side of her because it was then that I realized that Doug and I needed to go our separate ways for a while.

So there I was a couple of months later in his living room and Doug was worse than the night we had our blow up. I have no idea what we talked about that afternoon sitting next to his terrible little Christmas tree, but it was the last time I remember Doug as an angry young man. That summer he went away and when he came back Doug had changed. He came back and he loved people, he loved life and he loved Jesus. He began to make amends to the people he had hurt. He apologized to professors at the college and he told all of his drinking buddies that he still loved them, that he would still be there for them but that he could no longer party with them. The years that followed marked the most remarkable change in a person that I have ever witnessed.

His drinking buddies tempted and tempted him but he continued to say no and love them at the same time. If his buddies got in trouble it was Doug they called. I remember one night after we had graduated. It was Homecoming weekend at the college and several of his old drinking buddies came back to town. He was a year removed from his old life but after the game those guys still asked if he wanted to go have a drink with them.

"No," Doug said with resolve. "I have to go home and study my Sunday school lesson for church tomorrow." Doug was a Sunday school teacher and his friends respected him. If those guys were ever going to visit a Sunday school class Doug was the type of teacher they

EVERYTHING ELSE

wanted. Doug became a youth pastor and shaped and mentored young men. Doug poured himself into others, ultimately mentoring the son of the Dean of Students. The same Dean of Students that he had threatened to beat up one evening at school. I have no idea where all of his old buddies are today, but Doug does, because from time to time they still call him when they need to hear from someone they know loves them. Doug is now a dorm parent at the same college we attended together and has an incredible wife and an amazing little boy.

Doug is still one of my closest friends. There is not a month that goes by that we don't talk on the phone. Doug tells me about the young men he is pouring his life into- and most of the time it is the athletes, the ones that the Bible majors are maybe a little afraid to get close to. There are many people that talk about mentoring, they go to school to learn how to pastor a church, they read books about it, but Doug actually does all of the things that people write books about. I like remembering the way Doug used to be because it is a reminder to me that God can change the heart of anyone and can pour light into the deepest darkness. Doug used to be one of the scariest guys that I knew, but now he is one of the kindest and gentlest. If you met Doug today and I told you about the way he used to be you would call me a liar, but Doug, Ryan, Amy and I know the truth. We all know that God changes hearts. He turns terrifying into beautiful.

EVERYTHING ELSE

Robbers, Friends and Newlyweds

The first Christmas of a married couple will set the tone for most Christmases to come. It has to be that perfect blend of fun and touching, romantic and humble, just enough but not too much. The first Christmas that we shared together was going to be unforgettable.

We were in our first house, and we took our time picking out the perfect Christmas tree; no artificial tree would do for us. We wanted the real deal with the needles on the floor and the amazing aroma that only a real tree can bring to a home. We purchased it and made our way home, visions of matching sweaters and evenings sipping hot cocoa next to our picture perfect tree replaced the visions of sugar plums and danced in our heads. We put it into the stand and promptly set about realizing the impossible dream: getting the Christmas tree to work. We worked for hours to get that sucker up, but no matter what we did it wouldn't do right.

It wouldn't stand up straight… for anything. I'm not a handy man, but I can improvise so we set the tree up in a corner with a window on each side, tied string to the tree trunk and then pulled it

EVERYTHING ELSE

tight to the left so it would stand. We had nothing to tie the string to to keep the tension on it, so to keep the tree upright we ran the string out the window then shut the window on the string to keep it tight. It was beautiful, even with the incurable lean.

We set a budget for gifts and both of us went out and spent way more than what we had allowed. We were newlyweds and we didn't have much money so we wrapped the gifts in the exact same wrapping paper because we couldn't afford two different kinds. We used post-it notes that we had as nametags for the packages. We spent Christmas Eve with Amy's family and then came home so that we could wake up on Christmas morning and have our own little Christmas. We made a little makeshift bed in the living room floor by the tree and kept the tree lights on all night. It was so special. We awoke on Christmas morning like two little kids. We couldn't wait to give each other the gifts that we had spent so much time picking out. My beautiful new bride would be the first to open her gift. I picked up the package that had her name on the sticky note and handed it to her. She began to open the gift and once inside the box realized somehow the sticky note had gotten messed up and what she had opened was actually one of her gifts for me. She then handed the gift off to me, I finished unwrapping it and got the gift. I was, by count, half of a turn ahead of her.

This was not part of the perfect Christmas plan. I didn't know what to do. There was nothing in the Christmas Rule Book under the subheading of gift exchanges that dealt with this issue. So she grabbed another one that had my name on it.

"Here, open this," she said. I got about half way through before I realized it was actually one of my gifts for her. I handed it off to her and then she got a half of a turn. We not only caught up but we broke even because every time one of us thought we were opening our gifts, it was really the gift for the other. The tags had all gotten

EVERYTHING ELSE

messed up. This little game went on through all of our gifts. Every name tag on every gift was wrong. We discussed how weird it was, but in the spirit of Christmas it quickly became a nonissue. It was not until about a year later, when my friend Ryan, who was prone to pranks, was over for dinner that the topic resurfaced. After some small talk, he turned the conversation to our first Christmas, nearly a year in the past at this point.

"So last Christmas… were your gifts okay?" Then it started to make sense. The weekend before Christmas Doug and Ryan did some housesitting for us while we were out of town. Ryan relayed the story of how, before Amy and I got home, he and Doug had taken the sticky notes with our names on them and switched every gift. But this was not the cruelest of all jokes that Ryan would play on this newly married couple.

Amy and I could not have been married more than a month. It was late and I was having trouble sleeping. We were living in the apartment Ryan and I had shared before I got married, but not wanting to be the ultimate third wheel he moved out. So there I was, lying in bed, wide-awake when I thought I heard something scratch on the window above our bed. At first I just thought my mind was playing tricks on me, but it kept getting louder and more intense. I lay there and reasoned out every single sound that it could possibly be: it could be the wind… if it was windy. It could be a bush… if only there was a bush by the window. It could be a huge, scaly bug stuck between the pane and the screen…

There's something you should know about me: I am a pansy, a 100-percent, plant-me in-the-garden-and-water-me-every-other-morning, pink and "yeller" pansy. Amy has to kill the bugs. One time, we thought someone was in our garage. Amy and I both jumped out of bed and I began to hunt for a weapon to protect me while I hunted for the phone to call 911. When I finally found my weapon and phone I looked up to find that Amy was not in the room

"Amy?" I ninja-whispered as I crisscross-tucked through our house looking everywhere for her only to find that she had already gone into the garage, out of the garage door and was searching the yard for whoever might have been in our house. I meanwhile was still in the house clutching a bat and the phone. So there I lay, in bed, listening to the sound of whatever was outside our window growing louder and louder and doing nothing. I contemplated just popping up, real quick-like and looking out the window, coming face to face with the last memory I would have on this earth before whatever was out there with its gnarly fingernails, or possibly even knife-like talons, raking across my bedroom window. But I have seen too many movies where a look out the window ends in nothing but body parts, everywhere. So... I just lay there, praying it would go away. It did not.

Finally I thought to myself, "Brett you are the man of this house, you married this woman promising to protect her, so do something!" Just about the time I got my courage up, I remembered that if you did not get the back door latched good it would swing open during the night. When Ryan and I lived in the apartment we had many mornings where we would wake up and the back door would be wide open. What if someone or something is out there and the back door is open? They (or it) will come right in... It was time to do something, so I slowly got out of bed. I had only been more terrified once before that moment and I was so terrified at that moment that the other moment escaped me. I could barely get my legs to move. I made my way out to the hallway and through the kitchen and I could see that the door was closed, but was it latched? Was it locked? I made my way all the way to the back door, grabbed the handle and breathed a sigh of relief as it resisted; it was locked.

EVERYTHING ELSE

Then it happened. Our front door was on the opposite side of the apartment, directly across from the back door. You could look directly through the kitchen and living room to the front door, which I did and that is when I saw that the front door handle was moving back and forth. And just like that, ladies and gentlemen, there was a new number one most terrifying moment of my life. I stood there, frozen to the old linoleum floor and watched as the handle jiggled back and forth. It was official; we were victims of a full-on domestic assault. Whoever it was had moved from our bedroom window to the front door. I knew that now was the time for action, the time when men were made. There was only one problem: I was officially in full-on panic mode. I quickly hacked into the databank of all the things I have stored away for just a moment such as this: tactical maneuvers, outsmarting the criminal mind, protecting the woman and not ending up on one of those true crime shows. Unfortunately, my databank was comprised of movies that have taught me that some criminals will innocently break in and rob the house and leave! No harm no foul! But if they saw me seeing them then I would be a witness and I would sleep with the fishes... I knew that whoever was on the outside needed to know that there was someone in this house. If I'd had a gun I needed to cock it so they would hear that sound and run. But I had no gun. If I'd had a sword I would need to swish it through the air so they could hear the sounds of ninja glory. But I had no sword. I needed a deep Goliath-type voice to say something manly, but I was so scared I could not speak. I just stood there staring at my front door handle jiggling back and forth and I was mouthing the words "Get out of here," but was literally so scared nothing but air came out.

I was failing at this whole marriage thing. The robber would come in and kill us both and I would go down in history as the most pansy of men, struck down standing at the back door making awkward squeaking sounds and completely unable to move. I couldn't speak, I

EVERYTHING ELSE

had no gun, no sword and no voice, but I knew that the person on the other side needed to know that this house was occupied, so I did the only thing that came to my mind. I took off in a dead sprint towards the front door clapping. I mean really clapping, loud, the type clap that could only come from some sort of scary monster that claps instead of growls. I was sprinting and I was clapping, I reached the front door and as hard as I could I slapped the door.

I was golden. I had slapped the door. I was brilliant. Think about it: if you were a burglar and you were trying to break in, standing on the outside and all of sudden you heard clapping, that would have to be scary right? After I slapped it, I stood there. Then I heard uncontrollable laughter on the other side of the door. I looked out the window, still confused as to what was going on, and there, standing at my front door was Ryan and his current girlfriend who happened to be Amy's best friend from high school. I was so angry that I wanted to fling open the front door and take a swing, but there was an issue with that scenario as well. Not only did I not have a gun, a sword or a voice, I wasn't wearing a stitch of clothing. I had done all of this in my birthday suit. Part of me really wishes that I had gone out there that night naked just to give them a little scare, but I was afraid that would only end in laughter as well. I grabbed a pair of shorts, threw them on and went out the front door still mad.

I had a few choice words for Ryan and his girlfriend, none that I would be proud of my children reading or hearing. Then I hear the sweet voice of my sweet, delicate wife resonating through our well-protected apartment.

"What are you doing? Why are you clapping?" Amy slept through every single moment, except for the part where her husband ran naked and clapping through the house. How was I going to explain this to her? How I heard these sounds and that love overcame fear and made me get out of bed? Love for her, with complete

EVERYTHING ELSE

disregard for myself, because I was the man of the house even though I was still quite willing to put the covers over my head making sure no appendages were sticking out, because everyone knows if you leave an arm hanging out the Boogie Man can grab it. You have to be careful to have everything covered. But no! Because of love I got out of that bed, naked, and went to face whatever foe might be awaiting me. Love caused me to clap when fear had taken over my voice. Love, woman! Love! And now you're mad because I woke you up clapping? Clapping for love, clapping to save your life, heavy sleeper?

Amy, since that time, has come to grips with the reality that if someday we are faced with a life or death scenario she will go first because I will be under the covers awaiting my princess charming to come rescue me.

Ryan went on to get married to a beautiful woman and they share four beautiful boys. I was there when they had their first. We had the chance to work at a church together and through that relationship Amy and Ryan's wife have become best friends. His youngest son and my son are best friends and I couldn't be happier. Ryan is a great leader; he sees things for what they are. He is slow and methodical in decision-making. He is an amazing worship leader. He is so talented in so many things, but his greatest attribute is friendship. If his youngest son, Cade, can be half the friend to my son that Ryan has been to me, then Graham will be better for it. Friendships aren't here just for us to have a few good laughs together; that is just a perk. The real purpose of friendship is to make us better. When I first met Ryan, I was a kid who lacked confidence and he taught me what true confidence is. Ryan has walked through some tough times in his life the right way, admitting when he was wrong and I have watched that and learned. I have learned how to be a leader from Ryan and I have learned how to love by watching Doug. I have seen what devotion looks like by living with my incredible wife.

These three relationships have formed, and are still forming me. Along the way, I have made more friends like Nate and Todd, some of the most creative and gentle people God has put on this earth. I have seen what being a man truly is by watching the way they encourage people and create amazing things that point people to Jesus. I overheard two dads bragging one time about how many of their kids' baseball games they have almost been kicked out of. It struck me at that time that when Jesus talks about love and kindness being the important thing, that we instead celebrate manliness as being crude or mouthing off or almost getting kicked out of baseball games. Why do we not celebrate what Jesus celebrates? Gentleness, kindness, love and encouragement are all greater virtues and deeper marks of manliness than spouting off profanities at little league umpires. All of these men in my life have shown these to me and my family and that is what I think true manliness is: giving yourself up for others, like Jesus going to the cross for us. I am forever grateful to these men. One prayer that I pray aloud with Graham every night is that he would grow to become a kind man and that he would love others. I celebrate with Graham anytime he shares with me how he went to sit and eat his lunch with a kid no one talks to. That is what makes this dad's heart pump a little deeper in my chest and makes tears well up in my eyes. When I remember the important people in my life, not one of the memories is how they fielded a ground ball or caught a football. Every one of them is about how they have loved my family and myself. So go, sprint naked and clapping! Be a man and encourage someone! Now, if you will excuse me I need to go rip a belch so I can regain my man card...

EVERYTHING ELSE

Bees, Lies and Nanny-Nanny Poo-Poo

I earned a degree in elementary education from that small college in Hannibal. I would love to say that I went into the teaching profession because of my passion for wanting to shape young minds, but to be honest, I looked at all the options for a degree and elementary education seemed to be the easiest. I would see those elementary ed majors carrying crayon boxes and poster boards down the hall and I thought back to how much I used to love art class in elementary school. Plus when I was hungry crayons made a great snack, especially when you washed it down with some Elmer's Glue. The idea of having my summers off also sounded pretty good to me. I found out that majoring in elementary education was a little tougher than I thought and apparently eating crayons in college was frowned upon. My wife was also majoring in education so we shared many of our classes. Amazing how once I got into a class with Amy my grades got better. She did not want to be dating a slacker.

Once I graduated, I got my first teaching job in a small Lutheran school. I was teaching first and second grade in a combined

EVERYTHING ELSE

class. It was a small school, so there was no music, phys ed, or art teachers. I was responsible for all of these subjects. I had about 12 kids. I had no idea what I was doing, but my class had a lot of fun. I feel the need to apologize to those kids now because there is no doubt that for the years that followed they probably struggled catching up with kids who had normal teachers.

I was the fun teacher. I was young and had energy. I didn't stand around at recess talking with the other teachers when I could be playing kickball. When recess was over, I was just as hot and sweaty as the all little boys in my class. It was during my time in the classroom that I discovered my aversion to chalkboards. Mainly because they are scary and they represent the many, many things that we don't know (and by "we", I mean me). I was student teaching in a second grade class standing in front of a chalkboard. I am not sure what we were doing, but I was writing the words kids would say on the board. One kid said "dryers" and I got the "dr" part down, then it hit me that I had no idea how to spell it. I was caught between the great question is it "iers" or "yers?" So there I am just standing there with this chalkboard stretching out for miles, with the real teacher sitting in the back of her room with her notebook evaluating my every move. I began to pray for a fire drill or a vomit emergency; anything to get me out of this situation. I am not sure which combination of letters I went with, but I wrote one of them down thinking to myself, "they are second graders, maybe they won't notice if it's wrong and hopefully the real teacher will have mercy on me it's wrong." I think I got a "C" evaluation for my student teaching so I am guessing that I made more than one spelling mistake.

It was in the classroom that I had my first experience with the bluntness of children. They don't understand tact, probably because when you are young and the world is so big and ready to welcome you, you just don't have time to understand tact. I had one student

EVERYTHING ELSE

who climbed the monkey bars and perched on top as I was below him. It must have been the first time he noticed my thinning hair.

"Mr. Laxton, you sure look young from the front, but on the top you look old." This was not an update to me and was probably one of the many teachable moments I chose to ignore.

In the small Lutheran school, everything was up to me. My students were mine from the moment they walked into the classroom. We went to recess with them and we ate with them. Since it was a small school, we had one lady who cooked for the whole school and she was an amazing cook. Within the walls of that building is possibly the only time ever in a school that you actually wanted to eat the school lunch, (unlike public school, unless they are serving the square pizzas... those were yummy). At this small Lutheran school they had a rule at lunch that the kids had to try everything on their plate. For one of my students, Joe, this was not an issue. He ate everything, except one thing: corn. Who doesn't eat corn, especially in the Midwest? Corn is a staple. You can play in a cornfield, then cut it down and eat it. I wish more things in life were like corn...

I was making my round around the lunch table when I saw the corn on Joe's plate untouched.

"Joe, you have to eat your corn." He just looked at me and satisfied that because I had spoken, he would now eat it, I kept on walking. About ten minutes later I walked past Joe again and still his corn was untouched.

"Joe, you know you have to eat your corn." He just looked at me and then gave me the international sign for "I have a secret." He waved for me to bend down as he put his hand around his mouth I put my ear up to his hands.

"Mr. Laxton I can't eat corn; it makes me loose." After hearing this I made an executive decision that Joe did not have to eat his corn.

EVERYTHING ELSE

I also found out that what you say to a kid is the truth, even if you were making something up or trying to make a bad situation better.

One day, on the playground, one of my little students, Stephen, was on the swings and was beginning to have a melt down because a wasp was buzzing around him. "Stephen, if you just sit still and leave it alone, it will leave you alone," I told him with great confidence in the fact that I was lying. As adults, we know this is not the truth. As adults, we know that if there is an insect, a cobweb or sometimes a leaf dive-bombing your head, you immediately turn into a ninja fighting an invisible enemy and everybody is suddenly kung-fu fighting. You never just sit there. If a bug sneaks up on you and crawls on your shoulder, the moment you notice you go into seizure mode and start flapping at it like an epileptic octopus.

I lied to Stephen for his own good, because I was just trying to get Stephen to settle down. Stephen never listened to me, mostly because Stephen knew that as a second grader, he was smarter than me. One time he brought up a math sheet that he was confused about. I looked at it and tried to explain to him what he had to do but he kept arguing with me.

"But Mr. Laxton, it says…" I cut him off, not giving him a chance to finish. We kept up this banter: me explaining how I was the teacher and I knew how to do it; Stephen trying to explain I was wrong and me cutting him off. He finally walked away from my desk and as I looked at his paper, it hit me that he was right. What I was trying to tell him was wrong.

He got about five steps from my desk and I knew I had to tell him that I was wrong. In adult conversations and arguments if you admit you were wrong, it normally brings some peace, some resolution, the whole grown-up aw-shucks forgiveness bit, but that is just not the case with kids.

EVERYTHING ELSE

"Hey Stephen, you were right," I said, because I'm the grown up and that's what we do. We admit when we are wrong and we move on. Stephen immediately whipped his little head around and stared back at me with a glare.

"See! I told you so!" It was like nanny nanny poo poo. He nanny- nanny poo-poo'd me!

So here I am on the playground with Stephen going crazy and the wasp pestering him. I told him to just sit still and to my surprise he did. Not two seconds later that wasp landed right on his ear and stung him. He jumped up and screamed, but I am not sure it was the sting of the wasp that hurt him as much as it was the sting that I had lied to him. He jumped up running and yelling and whipped his little head back at me once again to call me out.

"You lied! You said if I left it alone, it would leave me alone. You lied."

As a parent this story brings to mind some uncomfortable truths. One is how much the words that come out of our mouths mean, not only to children, but to anyone who is standing in the wake of those words. I have been guilty of saying things that I shouldn't have said, of speaking in the heat of the moment or yelling sometime my words come out without me thinking about the incredible truth that our words are "truth" to our kids.

Truth is more than a one-dimensional concept. Truth has a million dimensions and the truth that comes out of a mouth comes in words, comes in volume, in tone, in gestures, in facial expressions and in the context of where I am and who I am with at that time. I heard it said once that as parents "we set the volume level for our homes." If I am yelling because I am upset, my kids will grow up believing it is "normal" or "okay" to yell when in an argument or that yelling is the best way to be heard.

EVERYTHING ELSE

    I also think about the importance of those three little words: "I was wrong". Most of the time my pride makes it very difficult for these words to come out. I may know I am wrong, but I don't want to be nanny nanny poo poo'd from someone. I don't want to have it rubbed in. I am not sure that there are any better words to bring a heated argument back down to a simmer than a simple "I am sorry" or "I was wrong". I want my kids to know that the words "I am sorry" or "I was wrong" are some of the bravest, most important words they can use in their relationships. I want my kids to know that being right is not the point; that resolution is the point and healthy relationships are the point. But I also want to teach them that if they have exhausted all other options, that if they have tried to make whatever situation better, and if they have apologized if they were in the wrong, to give nanny-nanny poo-poo a shot; it might at least get a laugh.

EVERYTHING ELSE

Marriage and Family

Amy and I have been married for 17 years now. We have two children: a beautiful ten year old daughter, Tyler, and an eight year old son, Graham. And yes, we know that Tyler is a boys' name and if you ever happen to meet Tyler and call her "Taylor" she will correct you before it is out of your mouth. She is just like her momma. She looks like her momma and acts like her momma. She is super-creative and super-outspoken. She will tell you if you have bad breath or if she likes your outfit or not and you don't even have to ask her and most of the time she will tell you out loud. Our son, Graham, is all-boy he invents ways to injure himself and loves adventure. He is much more driven than I was at his age and he does well in school because school, for him, is competition. Graham has two loves in his life: baseball (namely the St. Louis Cardinals) and his momma. He calls his momma "his love." Tyler and Graham are typical brother and sister. They argue and fight sometimes, but sometimes they even find adventure together.

One summer we went on vacation to (wait for it...) Wisconsin. I am not sure you will find Wisconsin in any exotic

EVERYTHING ELSE

vacation pamphlet anywhere, but we had a reason. Amy's father grew up on a dairy farm in Wisconsin and her aunts still lived there and ran the family dairy farm. The kids had never met Amy's aunts and uncles. Understand the history behind his namesake: "Graham" was Amy's maiden name. When we were thinking of names for our little boy, I wanted a way to honor her family. She has three older brothers and a sister that passed away. I loved her family and thought that naming our son after them would be a perfect way to honor the part of his heritage that comes from his mother.

We arrived on the farm and it was pure adventure from the get-go. We met one of Amy's aunts who started touring us around the farm. We took off walking through an expanse of land with Graham, who was four at the time, running in front of us. All of a sudden, Graham threw his hands up in the air, slowly turned around and ran back to us, screaming the whole way. He reached us and we dropped to the ground looking him over and frantically asking what was wrong. Still screaming, he lifted his shirt to reveal a straight red line across his chest. Amy's aunt's eyes flew open at the same moment her hand flew to her mouth. "Oh my gosh!" she practically whispered, I forgot to turn off the electric fence." There was one single wire strung across the field meant to keep the cows in the field and Graham had found it, the hard way. Graham began to settle down and asked us what stung him. We did our best to explain the concept of the seemingly invisible wire holding a current of electricity; it's not easy to explain that concept to a four year old. For the rest of that trip, on and off he would again raise the question of what had stung him. To this day I am not sure he understands what really happened.

While on the farm, Tyler and Graham got to feed calves and milk cows, which for city kids was exciting and gross at the same time. They slept in a farmhouse and tried to ignore that special aroma that can only come from hundred or so cows and the thousands of cow patties in the field. But the highlight for them was our trip to the Wisconsin Dells. While there, we went to see a show that had everything from singers, to comedians and jugglers and the most amazing Chinese acrobats. They contorted and bent their bodies in ways that most human bodies couldn't achieve. The end of their act was an aerial artist featuring a woman who climbed up two pieces of red silk fabric. She would wrap herself in the fabric 30 feet in the air, wrapping the fabric around her body, arms and legs. Then she would let go, spinning as the fabric that was wrapped around her body would release and she would catch herself right before crashing into the ground below. This made an impression on Graham and Tyler, although Amy and I had no idea how big that impression would be.

We made our way home back to Lee's Summit, MO, near Kansas City. The next day started off like any other: I went to work and the kids went to playing. In our backyard we had a huge tree house about ten feet in the air that my father had built. Through the middle of this tree house was a hole in the floor with a rope that hung from the rafters to the ground, kind of like a fireman's pole. With the images of these Chinese acrobats fresh in their minds, they decided it was time for them to give it a whirl, so to speak.

Graham convinced Tyler to wrap the rope around his body, around his legs, around his arms and then around his neck. Graham jumped. Amy was in the backyard with the kids, on the phone, supervising, but having absolutely no concept of what the two had planned. When Amy turned around to check on them, Graham had already made his jump. The rope had untwisted from all of his body parts except his neck. She turned around to see her four year old son dangling helplessly from a rope and her daughter standing helpless above, not knowing what to do to help. Amy threw the phone and ran over to him, hoisting him up with all 5'3" (she'll say she's 5'3.5") to release the tension on the rope, which she succeeded in doing, but she

EVERYTHING ELSE

couldn't release the rope. She let go of him quickly and ran to go get one of the lawn chairs in our yard to stand on, providing the boost in height she needed to save him. Graham ended up with an incredible story and a horrendous rope burn around his neck.

A couple of months later, we were talking after a church service. Tyler began to talk about sin and the bad things that we do sometimes. I was trying to see if she understood the whole concept so I asked her to tell me what sin was and what was something bad she had done while assuring her that whatever she revealed would not get her in trouble. She sat thinking, tapping her lips with her index finger saying "hmmm, hmmm". Graham, a mouthful of mashed potatoes, interrupted her train of thought without missing a beat. "I know," he said talking through his taters. "You wap my neck with a wope."

I tried to explain to them that I did not believe that was sin and that they were trying something out that they didn't know was going to be dangerous. I wish there was some deep spiritual lesson I could draw from this experience, but there isn't. It was just kids trying to have fun and I think that is acceptable. And though the lesson isn't deep, it is relevant: fun can sometimes equal danger and innocence can end in pain. We want our kids to be careful, but sometimes the best teacher is experience. And sometimes, hindsight leads to laughter that isn't there midstream, so to speak. There are some people that I encounter that take everything so seriously. I want to tell them that a smile and a laugh could really help them out and that being so uptight all of the time is a waste of time. But at the same time, people need to be careful and cautious of variety shows in the Wisconsin Dells; they can lead to dangerous outcomes.

EVERYTHING ELSE

Cardinals, Mud Day & a Fun Sucker

I have a confession to make, something that most people don't know about me. My wife knows, and maybe a few others. It's in my past, and I don't talk about it much, mainly because I consider it a battle that I am still fighting. I will tell you… but you cannot judge me. I am a "NO" person. Yep! It's true. The word "no" lives just underneath my tongue, ready to jump out whenever I am asked a question.

"Can we have ice cream?"

"No.

"Can we go to the park?"

"No."

"Can we?"

"No."

I never noticed this until Amy brought it to my attention years ago. "Why do you say 'no' all the time?" Then she hit me with the hammer: she called me a "fun sucker." There are a couple of things about being called a "fun sucker" that bother me. First, it implies that I suck the joy out of everything, which I don't; I just kind of put the

EVERYTHING ELSE

quietus to the joy in the first place. Second, if you say it repeatedly, eventually you are going to say it so quickly that it sounds like you are saying something for which your mother would have washed your mouth out with soap.

Amy is a "yes" mom. She says, "yes" much more than she says "no". That makes her a "fun instigator" or a "funstigator." I like to think we balance things out. One spring afternoon she said "yes" and funstigated an annual tradition in our family.

In our backyard stood one of the most incredible feats of modern science ever: an adult-sized inflatable pool. When filled, it would end up being about four feet deep and probably ten feet across. The kids didn't know this was the poor man's aboveground pool. They loved it. They spent many a summer day splashing around in it feeling rich and cool and cool and rich, which is how every kid should get to feel in the summer. Then, as the days would cool down, we would prepare the pool for storage by letting the water out and deflating the pool for storage.

When we finally lifted up the pool, there was a perfect circle where there was no grass. Only dirt. Or rather mud. Well, actually a mud pit because of all the water we had just emptied out of the pool. The kids just stood there staring at the mud pit. If you have ever seen a snake charmer work his magic on a cobra and seen that cobra transfixed on the spot because of hypnotic rhythm, then you understand the way my children were looking at that mud pit. They looked up at Amy and they didn't even have to ask.

"Yes, but go put on your swimsuits." They dashed inside, made the change like Superman on an energy drink, and then for the next hour rolled around in the mud. They had mud in their hair, ears, teeth and, we found out later, in every, and I mean EVERY, single nook and cranny in their little bodies. When they were finished, we had them strip down right there in the backyard and we sprayed them

EVERYTHING ELSE

off with the cold water out of the hose. From then on it was an end-of-the summer tradition; the day the pool was retired for the season officially became "Mud Day."

After the revelation of Mud Day, I took some time to reflect on what Amy had said. "No" was my first reaction but I was going to improve on that. I didn't want to be a "fun sucker." I wanted to say "yes." Why am I sharing this? Because I want to share a victory we had as a family one summer, and it would have never happened if I said "no." We were in St. Louis, visiting family, and we started on our drive back to Georgia around one o'clock in the afternoon. We would hit home (and our beds) about midnight. The kids had the DVD cranked up and had already hit the zombie trance phase, minus the drool trickling out of the sides of their mouths. But it was inevitable. As we were driving through St. Louis, we drove right by Busch Stadium, home of our favorite baseball team, the St. Louis Cardinals. Busch Stadium was buzzing as there was an afternoon game getting ready to start. Amy made the comment that we had to do a better job planning so we could catch a game sometime while were visiting. As Amy and I continued talking (kids with their headphones on), we realized that, as much as we love the Cardinals and as many games as we have watched as a family in our living room, our kids had never been to Busch Stadium. Our kids saw the Cardinals play when we went to Atlanta to watch them take on the Braves, but they had never been to historic Busch.

By this time we were ten minutes outside the city in Illinois already. But our brains were both working on a "yes" plan. We should just go to the game, turn this boat around and go. There were so many no's… We had an eleven hour drive, meaning we would get home at four in the morning and I had to work the next day. We didn't have tickets, and it was 106 degrees out that day. We needed to plan better. So many no's…

EVERYTHING ELSE

But there was something else happening in our hearts as parents that day. I started thinking about making moments with my kids and you only get one shot at that. I don't want to be the old man looking back thinking I should have made more memories. This was an opportunity... it wasn't about baseball and it wasn't about Busch Stadium. It wasn't the responsible thing to do, but it was the right thing to do, for me and for my family. Amy looked at me, her eyes questioning if we should take the chance.

I not only took the chance, I took the next exit and turned around with the kids still staring mindlessly at the video screen, oblivious to what was about to happen. As we started to drive back into the city, the kids still had no idea. They had their pillowcases over the windows to keep the blazing sun out of the back. We were literally driving in front of Busch Stadium when Amy turned around to look at Graham and Tyler. It took them about 15 seconds before they looked up from their travel DVD induced coma and realized they were being eyeballed. They both took off their headphones.

"What?" they asked. Then Tyler lifted up her makeshift curtain and a huge smile opened on her face.

"Are we going to Busch Stadium?" Tyler's voice was full of hope. Then I said it....

"Yes," I said, realizing that I had already swallowed the no and was merely holding the yes inside until I could let it burst out. I said "yes," and it felt good.

"Are you serious?" Graham was in total disbelief. Then they both screamed. To this day, thinking about my unexpected, completely unreasonable and totally called for "yes," I have goose bumps, because to us, to our family, that day was epic. We bought tickets from a guy off the street. We sat in seats that didn't match what our tickets said. We bought a souvenir cup. Our kids got St. Louis Cardinal bats. It was hot. We got home late. I was tired. And it was

EVERYTHING ELSE

awesome! As we drove home later, I replayed the day over and over. We created the perfect day for our family and for our kids. We gave them the kind of day that when they are grown up, both Tyler and Graham will look back on and shake their heads, laughing and realizing that yes, Mom and Dad were a little nuts, but so much fun.

As parents, say "yes" more than you say no. Maybe there is a story out there that begins with "This one time, when I said no…" but the great stories, the great moments, the great memories, they all start with someone saying "yes." You can't always say "yes", but say "yes" whenever possible. Psalm 63:3&4 - "Because your love is better than life, my lips will glorify you."

EVERYTHING ELSE

EVERYTHING ELSE

Momma Graham

I didn't give this section a funny title because there was nothing funny about what we faced in 2008. Amy grew up in Hannibal, Missouri, the boyhood home of Mark Twain. It's kind of ironic that now I love writing so much and I never went to see any of the historic landmarks of one of the most famous writers of all time while I lived in Hannibal. Amy grew up with one sister and three older brothers. Amy was the baby of the family by a long way as her oldest sibling was 13 years older than her. Amy's father worked away from the home in St. Louis, Missouri, and lived there during the weekdays. While her father had many good traits about him, he was not around much so when all the other kids left for school or got married it was just Amy and her mom. She was very close to her
mother. Amy was the girl that made good choices and never got in trouble; she always worked hard, and still does.

Amy would explain that all this came from her deep commitment to and respect for her mother; she never wanted to be what might be considered a disappointment. When Amy and I lived in

EVERYTHING ELSE

Hannibal during college and our first year of marriage, we were at her mother's house every Sunday for dinner. Amy's mom was a fun lady; she loved her family and her family loved her deeply. The first time I ever met her mom while Amy and I were dating is a day I will never forget. I knew Amy's mom lived alone and I also knew that she really liked Amy's last boyfriend (the one she broke up with to date me). So on my first meeting I knew I was behind the eight ball. I walked in and met her mom and the first thing I noticed was what I thought was a dog sitting in her lap. This creature was part Chihuahua and part gremlin maybe? It was short, fat, didn't like strangers and it loved Amy's mother, Mary Anne. As the night went on we talked and the dog never left her lap. It just stared at me.

At one point, Amy jumped up and began to slowly creep towards her mom while looking at Susie (the dog).

"Watch this," she smiled back at me and then began to say "I'm gonna get her" and slowly extend a hand towards her mom. The dog just sat staring and began to growl. Susie's lip began to curl, Amy kept creeping closer, and then the dog leapt from Mary Anne's lap and took off after Amy. Amy took off running and the dog, convinced she had kept Amy at bay, returned to Mary Anne's lap. Amy did this two or three times with the same result.

Knowing I had to get in good during this first meeting with her mother it occurred to me that if I could get in good with the dog, Mary Anne would love me, or maybe at least let me get a foot in the door. What better way than to play the game I had seen my beloved play with the playful Susie?

"Let me try…" I stood and started creeping toward Mary Anne, just as Amy had done.

"I'm gonna get her," I crept closer. So far so good with the endearment. "I'm gonna get her," I should have known better than to push my luck…

EVERYTHING ELSE

Susie growled and snarled and then finally leapt from Mary Anne's lap and took off running. I stopped where I had seen Amy stop, thinking this is the familiar area where the dog understands it was just a game and that no one was going to really hurt Mary Anne. But the dog did not understand, nor did she stop. Instead, she jumped up and bit me right in the crotch. I was mortified. The first time I am meeting my future wife's mother and her dog bites me in the crotch. To this day, I am not sure that I have ever heard a woman laugh as hard as Mary Anne did that day. Amy's mom grew to love me and I loved everything about her: her cluttered house, her Sunday afternoon meals, her laugh, her love of her family and people. She was a remarkable lady. I loved the fact that everyone was welcome in her home; if you were to ever visit their house there was no need to knock because the front door was always unlocked. Always.

By 2008, Amy and I had moved with our kids to Lee's Summit, Missouri, where I was a student pastor. Amy would make frequent visits back to Hannibal and I don't think a day went by that they did not talk on the phone. We tried to convince Mary Anne to leave Hannibal and move in with us, but Hannibal was her home; all of her friends were there as was her church that she loved dearly. Amy's mom loved her church so much that she even sang in the choir. Mary Anne may have been the worst singer I have ever heard, (right behind Amy), but that was dedication and love and she would not leave. Mary Anne never left. I came home one day to find Amy on the front porch, her body wrapped in panic. Amy doesn't panic; in fact, in the entire time we had been together, I had only seen that side of her twice. She met me on my way into the house. I was on the phone at the time, but knew enough of my wife to know that this took precedence.

"Something is wrong, I can't get hold of Mom," her voice was changed into an amalgamation of fear, panic and choking pain. "I

EVERYTHING ELSE

called the neighbors and they are over there. They said the garage door is open, but no one is coming to the door," Amy was explaining, grasping at whatever calmness she had left in her. "You have to call them again," Amy shoved the phone at me so I took it and dialed.

"This is Brett. What's going on?" It was Mary Anne's neighbor, who explained that her husband had gone into the house, but it didn't look good and they would call back in a moment. There is something about the inherent knowledge that something horrible is coming your way. The time between knowing and not knowing drags. But the suspicion, the suspicion that will soon be confirmed and converted into knowledge, moves fast. Through the heart, through the mind, right into the body, pulling the throat so that it is hard to speak, wetting the eyes so that the tears can't be stopped.

Amy was in the house pacing and crying. Her agony was my agony and waiting for that phone to ring was impossible. I couldn't wait any longer so I dialed again. I didn't want to dial the number; I didn't want to confirm our agony. I felt like I knew what was coming. Someone answered on the other end. "Tell me what is happening."

"Mary Anne is on the ground. I'm so sorry. She is dead."

We were in our bedroom. I stood while Amy stared at me. How do you tell your friend that HER best friend, her mother is dead?

"Amy, your mom is dead."

My words hit my wife like an invisible sledgehammer. She collapsed, screaming. The kids ran up to the room, not knowing what was going on, just knowing that their mother, who always said "yes", could only repeat over and over the word "no", as if she held some sort of power to stop the inevitable. I explained that Mary Anne, their grandmother, their mother's mom and best friend, had died. We all lay there on the floor, crying together, with each other and for each other, wrapped in confusion and pain. I called each of Amy's three brothers to tell them that their mother had died. It hurt my heart to

EVERYTHING ELSE

have to say those words over and over again, but my pain could not even compare to the pain and loss that had taken hold of Amy's heart.

After I had called each of her brothers and other family members I called Ryan, my best friend and husband to Amy's best friend, Amanda. I told him the news and to tell Amanda. Amanda called right back and I talked with her for a minute. At one point, Amanda asked if she could come over. I didn't know what to tell her because I thought we would be packing up immediately to make the drive to Hannibal. Thirty minutes later, the doorbell rang and I opened the door to Amanda, standing there with tears streaming down her face.

"I'm sorry. I had to come over; I have to give her a hug." Amy was already halfway to the door; she and Amanda embraced and cried over the loss together.

As I look back at that time, Amanda standing in the doorway is one of my fondest memories. She was being a best friend who hurt for her friend, who apologized for coming over in the middle of our hurried packing because she needed to embrace her best friend and give her the tangible support, the tactile connection they both needed.

Recently, a man in our congregation passed away. It is wrong to say that he was just a man; he wasn't just a man, but a husband, with twin girls in kindergarten and another daughter in fifth grade. Amy, the kids and I went over to his widow's house to visit with her and there beside her was her best friend. It reminded me of Amanda and all that she has meant to my wife. Amy and Amanda are an unlikely pairing, polar opposite in many ways but very much alike in others. I've observed the way their friendship has helped to shape the women that they are. I have watched two ladies help each other be better women, wives and mothers. It is a blessing to have friends who in the middle of terrible circumstances will stand at the door for the simple purpose of offering something that might be comforting in a

EVERYTHING ELSE

way that nothing else could. Thanks Amanda, and I love you, in a totally non-romantic way.

EVERYTHING ELSE

The Family Dog, a Fire & Church

Two years ago we faced a hard time in our family and again church and people I love surrounded us. It was a different church, but the same outcome. I was standing in the hallway of Journey Community Church in Evans, GA where I was working. I was talking to some co-workers when my phone rang. I looked at the caller ID and it was Amy.

"Our house is on fire, I am not there, neither are the kids. Betsy, our neighbor, called and told me. I don't know how bad it is." It was just like that… Amy spoke in one fast, long stream of words.

"My house is on fire," I took off running, leaving my co-workers where they stood. I later found out that they thought I was kidding until they saw me screech out of the parking lot. It was only about a five mile drive to my house and while driving, I played the "How Bad Could It Be?" game consisting of questions like: Is it small? Big? Where is the dog? Did I leave the coffee pot on? Did I make anybody mad? I turned onto the road that leads to my subdivision and from about a mile away I could see smoke rising

EVERYTHING ELSE

from my neighborhood and that's when I realized I had lost the game. I turned into my subdivision, but cars and a group of people wanting to get a look at what was going on blocked it. I got out of my car and ran the rest of the way up my road. When I topped the hill I could see it all. There was no roof to our two-story house; I could see right through where a roof should be in my son's room. I could see his bed.

There were three fire trucks; one with a fireman on a boom arm spraying our house, or rather what was left of our house. Another fireman approached me and asked me if this was my house.

"Did you get our dog out?" That was my answer to his question. Whitey is our white boxer. I got her without talking to Amy about the acquisition. Amy came home from work one evening and there I was sitting with this so-ugly-it's-cute white boxer. Soon she, like me, fell in love with Whitey. My family loves this dog. The fireman explained that they had not been able to get in yet to which I conversely explained exactly where Whitey's pen was. After they got the fire under control, they ripped off our garage door and went in to search for our dog. It seemed like forever and then the front door opened and a dirty, gray and wet Whitey came sprinting out the door. All that mattered had been saved. Amy made it home eventually with the kids and we stood there in front of our home hugging and crying.

When things had finally settled down we looked around to see countless people from our church standing in the street ready to do whatever they were asked. That night they took us shopping because when you lose everything in a fire you don't think about how you don't have a pillow, a toothbrush or any clothing other than what is on your back. As if my family having nothing left wasn't bad enough, we had one of our former students (who had come to intern at the church for the summer) living with us. She had just arrived the day before and all the clothes she had brought with her were also in the house. So we did what any solid American family would do: we went shopping. Don't romanticize it; it was a mess. How do you go shopping for what you need when you need everything? We were confused, to say the least. My wife even bought a swimsuit cover-up; (she didn't have a swimsuit and we weren't going on vacation, but none the less she had bought a cover-up. The question of where we would live was answered quickly; a family from our church had a fully furnished, finished basement and told us that it was ours.

That night as we got ready for bed, we all sat on the air mattress that would be our bed for the next three months. Amy and I talked to the kids, reassuring them that we would be all right and that we would have a home again. We talked about how blessed we were that no one was hurt. At some point, I turned the conversation to how our church had and was taking care of us and how that was the purpose of the church. I talked about church as a building, then I explained that the church is more than a structure, it is an infrastructure made up of people.

"Where was church today?" I asked them

"On the street in front of our house." Tyler looked up at me and smiled. How right she was! It was an incredible time as a parent for my kids to get to see the church in action. There are many people that I have encountered that dismiss God because of the way they view the church. Maybe someone said something to hurt them, maybe they read something about a pastor or church that did something they weren't supposed to do or maybe they don't like how they think the church treats "sinners." But the church, with all her blemishes, is still beautiful. I learned about her true beauty as I watched her care for my family through so many versions of loss

EVERYTHING ELSE

Waffles, Burps and Whoa

I love being a dad. It was like a light switch was turned on in my life the moment I saw Tyler. I finally began to have a better understanding of the title of "Father," not just as it applies to me, but also as it applies to God. To tell the truth, I could do without the birthing process itself, but in some sick, X-Files way, it was beautiful. One of Tyler's favorite shows is *A Baby Story*. It is unbelievable to me that there is a reality show where you watch total strangers during the birthing process. I barely made it through the births of my own two kids and all I had to do was stand there and not throw up on anything important. After watching my wife give birth to our kids, there are two things I am convinced of:

1. Women are so much tougher than men. Men are pansies and we only act tough because we know that we are not.
2. If God had designed us so the men have the babies, we would be extinct.

EVERYTHING ELSE

I remember when Tyler was just about to shoot out, (Amy would adamantly disagree with the use of the phrase "shoot out," but it's my book) the doctor, who sees like a million of these things a year, asked me if I wanted to watch the head crown. He was not talking about a tiara or a royal event. I handle blood and those types of things well, so I took a peek. I quickly became a self-taught man when it came to crowning. Crowning a queen, I'm in; baby crowning, NO! When Graham was born, they asked me the same thing. They barely got the question out before I shut them down like Blockbuster Video…

As a parent, I probably do more wrong than right; it's just the way of parenthood, I think, the nature of the beast. Kind of like the nature of the child is to be honest and honesty often results in embarrassment for the parent. They do things that you are absolutely positive you have never done or said in front of them and you are left standing there, heat rising to your face, ears flushing red wondering where that came from. Kids say things out loud because they have no filter. It's adorable and funny… when it is someone else's child.

Amy was at Wal-Mart one day and Tyler was in the grocery cart basket. They started to turn a corner and almost had a head on collision with a bigger lady who was in one of the motorized shopping carts.

"Whoa!" Tyler said as the two of them swerved to avoid the collision. She followed it up with the standard question.

"MOM, DID YOU SEE HOW PREGNANT THAT LADY WAS?" (Using caps proves to you that it was so loud that it was well within earshot of the un-pregnant lady riding the scooter.)

Another time, Tyler had a sore on her lip that required a doctor's visit. The doctor explained that she had a form of the Herpes virus and gave us some ointment for her lip. That evening

EVERYTHING ELSE

I had to make a run to Wal-Mart and I had both kids with me. Graham was at that stage of talking where he just repeated the one word in your sentence that stuck out to him. As we approached the checkout the clerk looked at Tyler.

"Honey, what did you do to your lip?" (They can't help you find the Styrofoam cooler from the sales ad, but they can spot a cold sore a mile away AND be kind enough to comment on it.)

"I have the Herpes virus." Tyler piped right up and explained to the overly-concerned cashier. I stood there not knowing what to say like I was stupid. Graham, of course, picked out the best word ever to repeat over and over and over and over again at Wal-Mart: "Herpes, herpes, herpes…"

I did not even respond to the clerk. I just swiped my card and left with Graham still announcing "herpes, herpes, herpes" like it was some sort of chant that we did at home.

One time we had a couple over to our house to have dinner (the same family whose home we stayed in after ours had burnt down). Brian and Dawn are great people with three amazing daughters and after we had the opportunity to live with them for a month or so we found out they were the quietest family we have ever been around. I mean, they talk and stuff, but they weren't the loud family that we are… crazy loud would best describe it. Dawn is a woman of manners. You mind your manners around her, you don't burp around her, and you say "please" and "thank you." We were doomed from the get-go. We have taught our kids manners and we have taught them that while bodily gases happen, they are not something to be celebrated. They may not be ready for those White House dinners, but they're not going to have to be harnessed and caged in order to be fed. Graham still eats with his hands more than with a fork and both of them still

EVERYTHING ELSE

laugh after some unfortunate sound or smell comes from one of them.

We are all enjoying dinner and up to this point Graham has been using his fork like a good boy and there have not been any odd smells or sounds, but that was all about to change. In the middle of the dinner, Graham let out the biggest burp I have ever heard from him his short life. It was the type of burp you push; this was no accidental gas leak. Amy and I sat there stunned and Graham giggled. Graham got sent to his room to eat alone that night. I wondered, as I removed my son and escorted him to his room, how Brian and Dawn were going to view the burp. I was certain they were going to believe that it was regular practice in our house. I mean, to get something that big out of something so small with that kind of resonance would, honestly, take practice.

Then there was the waffle incident during family movie night. The kids had gotten in trouble a day or so earlier for making a mess in the living room so we had barred all food from the living room. As we sat, Graham got up and went into the kitchen, returning moments later by hopping across the couch. Graham seldom uses the floor; he is more like a squirrel crossed with a monkey. His entire life is a game of "The Floor is Molten Lava." He plopped down next to me and we continued to watch the movie. Out of the corner of my eye I thought I saw Graham put something in his mouth. I looked over and he was as still as a statue, cherubic, really; just sitting quietly watching the movie, not chewing anything, no evidence that a crime had just had just been committed.

I shifted my attention back to the movie, then out of the corner of my eye I saw him put something in his mouth again but this time I caught a bit more than before. It was a waffle. There was no waffle in sight and I looked him up and down pretty good.

EVERYTHING ELSE

"Graham, are you eating a waffle?" He just looked at me. "Graham, where did you get a waffle?" Then Graham reached down the front of his pants and pulled out half of a waffle. Let me say it again, my son reached down the front of his pants and pulled out a waffle. As a parent, you know that occasionally words will come out of your mouth that you hadn't considered before. Questions such as "Why is the cat walking like that?" and "Did you duct tape your sister's earlobes to her neck?" are bound to come up. But what I was about to say, well, I'd like to think that it will have an impact on parents and breakfast food manufacturers worldwide.

"Graham why do you have a waffle down your pants?"

The obvious answer of course was that he was hungry, but I didn't give him enough time to explain.

"That is disgusting!" I faked my anger with a stern brow. "Go wash… well… go wash everything involved!" I tried to sound mad… I really did. He walked off and I looked at Amy, barely able to contain my laughter and mouthed my explanation, "He had a waffle down his pants!"

EVERYTHING ELSE

EVERYTHING ELSE

A Challenge

There are so many other stories that I could tell, but I just didn't know how or where to fit them in. There was the time that Cheez and I set a tree in my woods on fire and the fire department came out and had to cut it down. There was a small article in our town paper about it and everything and we were sure we were going to jail. At the time of the incident we were supposed to be working on a devotional that we were going to lead for our youth group but that wasn't as much fun as fire. We prayed quite a bit while the fire department was working on the fire with most of the prayers consisting of confession of deep sins and begging for God to give us one more reprieve. We both knew what happened to people in jail and we wanted no part in it.

Then there was the time as a student pastor, I dressed up as Santa Claus and accidentally sucked in a beard hair. I stood on a stage in front of 200 plus students hacking like a cat with a hairball. That was funny until the next day when I had to go to the doctor because I was still hacking and coughing. I ended up with pneumonia and the

EVERYTHING ELSE

knowledge that any foreign object in your lungs can cause pneumonia… no lie. I had a friend that accidentally sucked in Cap'n Crunch or a Cheerio or some other cereal and he ended up with pneumonia as well. But all of those are better than my friends' kid who was trying to make a blow dart gun with a straw and a needle. He accidentally swallowed the needle and they had to wade through his bathroom trips for a couple of days to make sure it passed.

There are so many stories, so many people, so many experiences and a loving God who I know must get a good laugh at times out of our adventures. So why do I write all of this? What does it all mean? Now that you have almost finished reading this, where do you go from here? Well… I am not sure.

I believe that my life, with all the experiences, good and bad, comes down to Jesus and relationships. I know what you are thinking: here comes the sermon. But don't tune out yet. I mean, you made it this far so you might as well finish. If you like reading and like crazy stories and you have not read the Bible you should give it a try. One of the reasons I believe the Bible is true is because no one could make up some of those stories one obvious example Noah's ark. You might read it and be skeptical… Seriously, I mean, two of every animal? Come on! But my biggest question would have to be about the poop. What about the smells?

But in the Bible, you will also read stories about a man named David that committed adultery, then murdered another dude to try to cover it up. Then you read that God calls him "a man after his own heart." I like a God that says "I love EVEN YOU." I like a God that in the midst of all of your hang-ups, bad habits and wrongdoings, says "I still love you." Recently I took to reading through the life of Jesus; the "Gospels" as they are called in the Bible. I wanted to try to read it as if I had never gone to church to try to go at it with no preconceived ideas of who Jesus was. What I found is that I really like Jesus. He

EVERYTHING ELSE

was propaganda-free. When others would say that the way to God was eating this or that or jumping through dogmatic hoops, Jesus came and started including everyone: the prostitute, the cripple, the religious and the normal. He was telling people that it wasn't about getting your words right or even making all the right choices. It was about your heart. In one story, Jesus is coming into town and everyone is cheering Him on and He knew that the hands that were waving palm branches and the voices that were singing Hosanna, would soon be shaking fists and yelling "kill him." And yet He still chose to come and meet with us. I like a God that looks at a heart like mine and says that He can make my heart just like that of David's, even when I look at my heart and say "impossible." I like Jesus, a lot.

We are made to be with people. The people that we have in our lives make the stories better and serve to make sure that the stories happened the way you remember. You can't take yourself too seriously; you are never going to remember to zip up your zipper every time or always get all of the salad out of your teeth, but when those times come, hopefully you have a friend there that cares enough about you to tell you. (But if those times do happen and you're on your first date with lettuce in your teeth or walk out of the bathroom and you remembered everything but your zipper, laugh and tell the world about it later.) I think people like a person that doesn't have it all together. Makes you feel a little bit better about yourself. So I guess what I am suggesting is that you be that person that makes someone else feel better about who they are. You don't have to stick your face in a head of lettuce, but it wouldn't hurt to be the person that you would want to be friends with.

One of the simplest teachings out of the Bible is "do unto others as you would have done to you." So simple, but so good. Imagine a world where everyone actually treated the other person the way they would want to be treated. A place where forgiveness is abundant, where people don't look at you funny or bring up your past. What if you lived so that you could make sure that when something happens and you are in someone else's story that you are the nice guy? What if you are the happy ending? I say to my kids all the time, "Just be nice." Can you imagine what it would be like if everyone would "just be nice." They say that nice guys finish last, but in my stories, in my life and in my memories, the "nice guy" always finishes first when it comes to things that count.

There's a very specific reason why I wrote this book, or rather why I gathered this collection of pieces of things that have shaped me, taught me and touched my heart. I wrote it for therapy and I wrote it to remember the things that have happened to me. I wrote it as a map to my past because I eventually faced something that I was afraid might take my past away from my future.

As I have mentioned before, my dad has a disease called NF2. It is hereditary; my brother and I both ended up with the same disease. Since high school, I have had MRI's to monitor these non-malignant brain tumors. In December of 2008, the doctors felt it would be best to go in and remove one of the tumors in an effort to preserve my facial function on one side. They weren't positive they could save my face from paralysis, but they felt there was a good chance they could and if I waited my chances of avoiding facial paralysis would diminish. We knew going into the surgery that I would lose hearing on the left side and that my balance would be messed up, but in January of 2009 I went in for brain surgery.

We had the surgery, and I say "we" because when going through something like this your spouse goes through just as much as you. The surgery went well; I don't remember much besides a wicked bad headache. During that time my church rallied around my family; they cleaned our house, fixed us food and visited us in the hospital. Below is a not that I posted on my Facebook page six months

EVERYTHING ELSE

following my surgery. The events were still fresh on my mind and I think it better explains my feeling than I would be able to do so far removed from it.

Things I Didn't Know Six Months Ago…

A little over six months ago, I had brain surgery and the other day I was thinking of all the things I know now that I didn't know, or maybe didn't know to the degree that I do now.

Six months ago I didn't know….
1. That God was this faithful.
2. A woman could be as beautiful as my wife was when I woke up.
3. That an elephant could be dressed as Batman (ask Kenzi).
4. I would like Jell-o as much as I did.
5. That my children don't care-they just love me.
6. That Tyler could tease me so much about my smile.
7. That Graham was fascinated by scars.
8. That Amy was so patient.
9. How much two good ears means.
10. How beautiful the body of Christ is.
11. How addictive podcasts are.
12. How much I would miss all my students at Raytown when I was gone.
13. That a tumor on the spine is much more painful (like crying painful)
   than brain surgery.
14. What the phrase "God is good" really meant.
15. That you can get used to being dizzy.
16. I was gonna walk like I was drunk.
17. That I could sleep so much.
18. How brave my mother and father are.

EVERYTHING ELSE

    19. *How brave Amy is... and continues to be.*

    20. *How much I would miss playing basketball.*

    21. *How hard it would be to play catch, (although Graham doesn't care   cause he is still gonna throw the ball 90 mph at my face whether I can see or not).*

    22. *How much I have been blessed.*

    23. *How Christ can be so close when we are so in need.*

    24. *How much it hurts when people tease about me not being able to hear very well.*

    25. *How many friends I have.*

    26. *I was joking about #24... just wanted to see if you were paying attention.*

    The list you just read is a growing list. Every day it expands, but only if I pay attention. And therein lies the issue, paying attention. How many times do we find ourselves in a conversation, in a meeting, on the phone, talking to our kids or spouses where the lips are moving, but we have no idea what they are saying because we are mentally somewhere else? Our minds are somewhere in another universe and if we are not careful, when we finally decide to pay attention, it's too late and the moment is over.

    I am thankful that in the midst of a very difficult time in my life I was made to slow down and pay a little more attention to what was going on around me. Nothing makes you more appreciative of life than the idea that you are going to lose it.

    The other day I took Graham to see a baseball game between the Angels and the Astros. Like I have said before, we are huge Cardinal fans but this past year Graham's favorite player was traded to the Angels so we wanted to take the opportunity to go see him play. Graham and I made plans to go early, to go to batting practice and maybe, just maybe, get David Freese's autograph. Graham obsesses a

EVERYTHING ELSE

bit and as soon as I told him that maybe we could get an autograph, I realized that to him, my "maybe" was as good as a promise. He was constantly talking about how we would get it, where it would be, what time it would be, what he would sign, all of the things that determine that something is "definite." As the days approaching the game dropped away, I was pretty nervous. I just knew if we didn't get his autograph Graham would be crushed. I prepared a "dealing with disappointment" speech and everything.

    The day arrived and Graham had laid out what he would wear; he had his Sharpie, a ball and his ball glove all laid out the night before. We arrived and waited as the Astros took some batting practice. They finally left and slowly the Angels players began to come out of the dugout. There were about 20 other fans around the Angels dugout and as the players came out to stretch and then back to the dugout to get their gloves people would call players over hoping for autographs. Most players just put their heads down and went into the dugout and then ran back out ignoring the fans. I don't have a problem with this as I understand players can't sign for everyone and the game is their job. Finally after what seemed like an eternity, David Freese came out and ran over to a VIP area that was roped off for some people more important than ourselves.

    I don't find myself praying for small things like autographs very often, but on this day it wasn't a small thing. This was a boy's dream. I said a little prayer and watched as Freese finished up in the VIP area and approached the dugout. The 20 or so fans that were there began calling out, "David! David!" as they held out caps and baseballs. David put his head down and took one step into the dugout, his body disappearing and only his head visible.

    "Mr. Freese!" Graham hollered out. I am not making this up David stopped and looked straight at a little boy holding out a ball and a pen. It was Graham. He looked right at Graham. Then David held

EVERYTHING ELSE

up his hands, the universal sign to throw the Sharpie and the ball to him. Graham threw a perfect strike to David. I took it all in. It was like a movie. He signed the ball and threw the Sharpie and ball back to Graham. Graham turned and looked at me after he caught the ball. It was like he was holding the equivalent to an adult million dollars, and while a million dollars would be nice, I wouldn't trade all the money in the world for that moment. That day Graham also got a batting practice ball from one of the Astro coaches and he caught a batting practice ball from Albert Pujols. It was more than I had asked for or dreamed of. As we left that day, Graham's pockets bulging from all the baseballs he gathered that day. I thanked Jesus that Mr. Freese stopped. One more step into the dugout and the moment would have never happened.

I tell you that last story because I want to challenge you to stop. Stop what you are doing and pay attention. We are taught many lessons in life intentionally. Potty training, how to write, how to read, how to catch a ball, how to eat, and the list goes on. But what about everything else? How to love, how to live, how to be thankful. We learn everything else in the moments in our lives when we aren't really paying attention and we need to pause and really listen in those moments. Pause and be thankful. Pause and make little mental notes. Pause and write down a story so that we can have them to share with others. So my challenge is for you to pause. For the next month, for the next 30 days write a story a day. Let's say you take my challenge, that for the next 30 days (or say 20 you can take Saturday and Sundays off). Write down a story from your life and a lesson that you learned from that moment. I think it will build a habit in your life to pause more often, to pause while in the moment of some big or small story and find the lesson in it that I believe Jesus desires to teach you. It will create in you a heart that is thankful in the big and small stories. What are the stories that taught you "Everything Else?"

EVERYTHING ELSE